THE FOREST STATIONS

William Fairbank

FRONTIER

Frontier Publishing
Kirstead
Norfolk NR15 1EG

First Published in Great Britain by
Frontier Publishing 1998
Reprinted 2004

ISBN: 1 872914 20 9

Associated Items

In association with this book are a folding booklet and a set of 15 postcards showing photographs of the same sculptures. Also available is a video film, 'The Forest Way', scripted by William Fairbank, and focusing on the spiritual and environmental issues behind The Forest Stations. For further information and sales, please write to the publisher at the above address.

Acknowledgements
Anthony Middleton, AM Photographic, Cambridge.
Theresa Fairbank, Technical section Part 1 drawings.
Gavin Brown, Technical section Part 2 drawings.
Emma, Sam and Alice Fairbank. Top models.
John MacDonald. Principal Assistant.

Typeset by T&O Graphics,
Bungay, Suffolk

PRINTED IN GREAT BRITAIN
by Crowes of Norwich

Introduction

The question comes again, “Why are you making the Forest Stations?”

A fundamental hunger in each of us centres on ‘breakfast, lunch and tea’ survival. Another great thirst is the yearning for knowledge which leads our brains to think and wonder: What is going on? Why is this happening? Why are we here?

Hold on… what’s the big deal? If we happen to be one of the many millions of fortunate ones in the world who have enough food, have a roof over our heads, warmth in the winter and a doctor nearby, what is the point of asking these questions? However interesting they may be, there are no clearly defined answers.

The artist in me has an insatiable desire to both ask the questions and to communicate my reactions.

Imagine we are all on the high street. Each of us has a shop and above my door is written, ARTIST. I head out and look and think and talk and ideas start to bubble inside my head. Returning to the studio I build a sculpture and put that sculpture into the shop window.

I see myself as a communicator, communicating ideas and feelings to others through these sculptures. Speaking to myself and saying it out loud in this book, potentially there is an exchange with everyone in the world, no matter their age, race, wealth or personal beliefs.

For me the attraction of the Stations of the Cross lies in the timeless nature of the subject. However, these are a present day set of stations, built in a time of environmental crisis with the world population set to double in the next thirty years.

From a timber perspective, if we wish to hand on fine timbers to our children and beyond, we must nurture an understanding and an appreciation of the value of trees, both while they are living and after they have been milled. The fact that we have to plant a tree today for it to become workable timber in 50 or 100 years time is becoming a harder and harder idea to grasp as we head into the new millennium. Forests are casualties to the ever growing demand for land space.

During my life I have appreciated the work of carpenters, cabinet makers and woodcarvers from all around the world and, following in these traditions, I have tried to work the timber to the very best of my ability. To some the interest of The Forest Stations lies in the craftsmanship, to others it may be the wood grain and whether or not you even read the titles is your own decision.

I invite you to view these sculptures with as open a mind as possible. I was drawn to this subject because the Stations of the Cross have always been about personal devotion and this means that each of our own views is unique, relevant and valid.

The Forest Stations are dedicated to beings of the world for whom timber plays an integral part in their lives.

William Fairbank, Norfolk, England.

www.williamfairbank.com

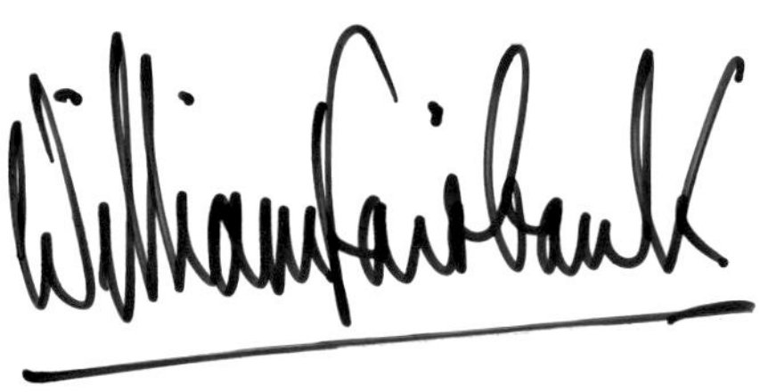

Minst's Tale

Not long ago, in a small, reasonably peaceful village, there lived a man called Minst. He owned all the land and most of the villagers worked for him.

Essentially Minst was satisfied in his life but he had one great unfulfilled ambition. This was to visit Jerusalem and see the place were Jesus had been crucified. Unlike anyone else in the village he also had enough money to embark on such an expedition.

Minst had made his way by land and by sea to Jerusalem and, in due course, he had returned home to his village. The fact that someone in those times had made such a long and dangerous journey and then returned safely to their village was a great sensation indeed. Communication was by word of mouth and soon after he returned he found himself in the market square, surrounded by the whole village, who eagerly awaited to hear about his journey.

The three priests sat at his feet and before Minst could start speaking the senior priest stood up and said how it was the hand of God that had guided Minst away from them and it was the hand of God that had brought him back. Certainly the whole village may have appeared quiet and respectful, but how they just bubbled with excitement!

Everyone had brought food to the meeting. Minst, who was a good and popular man, laid on three barrels of beer. "Come on Minst, tell us about Jerusalem. Did you see the place were Jesus was crucified?"

Minst started to speak. "I walked along the Via Dolorosa, which means the Way of Sorrows. At that time this was the path that all condemned criminals took and led to Golgotha, the place of the skulls. The executions took place outside the city walls. Jesus was condemned by Pontius Pilate and following his crucifixion he was laid in the tomb and yes, I did see the stone that had been rolled across the entrance."

It was quiet, very quiet for a moment as they all had their own pictures in their minds' eye. "Please go on", said one of the children.

"I will tell you what it is like. You are standing there at the place where the trial happened and I walked, just as Jesus had done, all the way from here to the place of execution and it is quite a distance."

"How far Minst? Can you describe it to us?"

"I am describing it to you," he replied. "Now don't you rush ahead. The distance was about the same as from here to that oak tree up on the hill. If you were running and there were no animals in the way then you would be there fast. But just imagine what it is like if you are in the middle of a city with narrow streets and there are crowds of people everywhere. The path leads out through a gate in the old city walls and winds up a rough track."

The tall priest, who knew the Bible story well, asked Minst about the place where Simon of Cyrene helped Jesus to carry the cross. "Look up there at the oak tree. Come back about half-way to that clearing by the old clay pit and that would be the place. But, as you can see, he still had some way to go after that. There are places all along the route and they are called Stations of the Cross. You stop at each one and at that one you say 'Praise be to Simon of Cyrene'. You say your prayers and then you go onto the next one."

It was then the turn of one of the other priests to question Minst. "It is all very well saying that Jesus was helped by Simon somewhere out there by the clay pit, but what happened between here and the pit and later, between the pit and the oak tree?"

"Well, it's strange but they have these extra Stations where other different things happened along the way. I know that they may not actually be written down in the new part of the Bible but they happened and the sites are all marked beside the little street along which they took Jesus. Look, I walked up and down so many times that I learnt all those stations so I will tell you just how I saw it."

1

"The First Station is called 'Jesus is condemned to death' and I really felt that I could see all the crowd of people there in front of Pilate and Jesus. There was this argument going on between Pilate, who was the Roman Magistrate and governor, and the people and the priests. It was so awful and yet in that moment I was also aroused! Yes this power came up at me and I tried to appreciate the feelings of Pilate as within himself, he saw no reason to condemn Jesus. I felt the real threat did not come from Pilate, but from the crowd who were so angry! I felt that the crowd thought that Jesus was too good for them and that is why they wanted him killed."

It was absolutely quiet around Minst in the village square and, when the people talked together afterwards, it seemed that most of them felt confused at this hate and aggression coming from within themselves. "Go on", said the priest gently, encouraging Minst, "Tell us, were you aware of the presence of Jesus?"

"Oh yes, of course he was there, I sensed that, at the time, he was detached and watching all this going on, as if it was inevitable. You see, I felt that if Pilate had not sentenced Jesus, the crowd was so angry they would have attacked the magistrate himself. He did not want to be responsible for the death of Jesus, but finally he gave way and in a very weak voice, he said that Jesus should die."

2

"Then the soldiers took Jesus and the Second Station was nearby. This was the place where they beat the poor man and then tied a beam onto his back. Those angry people were encouraging the soldiers to tie the beam on and beat him. Then they put the crown of thorns on his head. I must say that before I actually went to the place, I saw the soldiers as the bad people, but right then I sensed the aggression coming out of the crowd.

"If this had happened here it would have been you and I who were in that crowd and, if you want to know what I felt, it seemed to me that it was the people who were responsible. The soldiers were under orders."

The villagers empathised with Minst. It was as if they were all there with him in Jerusalem.

"That heavy beam was tied on with leather thongs and the crown of thorns was pushed down hard onto his head and blood ran down into his eyes."

3

"Then they had him ready for his final journey and, if it had been here, all that had taken place so far would have happened among us in our square. This was the time that they moved on towards the slope leading up to the oak tree. All the crowd were behind Jesus and they were shouting as if they had just won a battle. They were all following Jesus as he moved up that track running between my house and the store. It was when they were clear of the store that you come to the next Station which is called 'The First Fall.'

This is the first one which is not in the Bible, but when you see the place as I saw it, you would not be surprised that he fell at this moment. The pressure from the crowd who were behind him must have been overwhelming and he fell right over onto his face. Many in the crowd could not have seen that he had fallen and would have carried on surging forward.

As I look around in this square, I feel it as I felt it there in Jerusalem. I know that some of the younger men among us (and here Minst looked over at the lads who had already started drinking beer) would have been at the front of the crowd, even though they may not have had a real grasp of the reasons behind the crucifixion. Others may have been sorry for Jesus but would have been in the crowd just to see the spectacle."

4

"Each time that I walked along the Way of the Cross I experienced Mary's desperation. The next Station, the fourth, is called 'Jesus meets his mother'. They had a picture of her looking up at her son as he staggered past. I spent a long time looking at this one. I imagined her reaching forward to her son and, you know how you mothers will give the last food to your baby? – well I saw her reaching out and giving him energy so that he could pull himself together and move on.

Can you imagine how it was for me out there in Jerusalem? It is an extraordinary town and as one moves around, one is talking and dealing and making friends with all sorts of people. In Jerusalem the people were walking up and down the streets past these Stations of the Cross every day. Even though many were not Christians, they were very devout people. This Station, like the first fall, is not in the bible."

5

"The distances in Jerusalem are about the same as I have shown you here and if he had met his mother just before that old clay pit, he would still have only been about half-way to the oak, where he was going to die.

In Jerusalem I had tried to imagine how it had been. I think that the soldiers and leaders had started to worry because Jesus was going to die before he had reached the oak. That is why they pulled Simon of Cyrene out of the crowd and made him help Jesus. I am sure Simon really loved that man; he came forward and put his arm around Jesus and helped him along."

It was the leading priest who pointed out that if he was carrying the cross, then how could he put his arm around Jesus?

"No", said Minst, "I saw the cross beam tied to Jesus and Simon with one arm around him and the other holding onto the cross beam. Each of us hears and sees the Stations in our own way and each of us is right. The only truth is that Simon helped Jesus."

Perhaps the three priests disagreed with Minst's view, but they did not say anything else about it. Minst was well underway now and, to emphasise his point, he said that some people believed Simon had helped Jesus all the way to the cross. His own thoughts were that Simon only helped Jesus for a short while, and that this gave him the strength to carry on by himself.

6

"I have to say that as I walked along these Stations in Jerusalem, I became so aware of the anger of the crowd and how the shouting for his blood went on and on. It was then that he passed close by this woman Veronica. Without a thought for herself she took off her head scarf, stepped up to Jesus and wiped his face. For me this was a moment of great compassion. Tradition has it that the face of Jesus was left imprinted upon that piece of cloth. The anger of the crowd was directed at her as well as at him and, as she wiped his face, she was protecting him."

7

"Look there for a moment. Look at the oak up on the rise. The next Station would happen on that piece of flatter land just before the rise; it was just as Jesus was about to reach this ground that he fell over again. When I was in Jerusalem, I had a very strange experience as I rested by this Station."

There was silence in the village square as they all waited to hear about Minst's strange experience. At first no-one interrupted because he had an extraordinary dream-like look to his face. Then the elder priest said gently, "He was under so much pressure, he was being beaten by the Roman soldiers."

"No, No!" shouted Minst, "It did not seem like that to me. You see there was this corner and he fell, oh yes he fell, but the pressure did not come from the crowd. He fell because pressure forced him down but that pressure came from within himself. Ask the priests, they know the Bible. How many times was it written that this was going to happen to him? Jesus had said to the disciples only the night before that he was going to die. I felt that at this moment he fell down, but then he forced himself towards the cross. Such pressure."

8

"I want to help you all imagine just what it was like for those people in Jerusalem on that morning, as he was led towards the place of execution. In a way Jesus was leading the crowd, who were going to watch him being killed. Look at ourselves in this village, I am pretty sure that we all would have wanted to see the spectacle." Minst looked across at a group who were sitting on the ground. "With the greatest of respect, I really do not think that you would have been able to keep up with the crowd." Most were older women but there was a group of very young children playing nearby.

"If this had happened here I think that you women would have gone ahead and be waiting for Jesus, somewhere up there on the flatter ground, just below the oak tree. This next Station is in the Bible".

The younger priest was pushed forward by the other two and he quoted this passage from the Bible. 'And there followed him a great company of people, and of women who bewailed and lamented him. But Jesus turning unto them said, "Weep not for me but weep for yourselves and for your children. For behold the days are coming when they shall say, 'Blessed are the barren and the wombs that never bore and the breasts that never gave suck.' Then shall they begin to say the mountains 'fall on us' and hills 'cover us'. For if they do these things when the wood is green, what will happen when it is dry?"

In the village square there was absolute silence. Each person listened to these words and was deep in their own thoughts. At this point the atmosphere in the village can only be described as one of deep depression. An old lady whispered to her friend that she could not understand why Minst had gone all that way, and through all that danger, just to come back to tell us that we were all heading for bad and dangerous times. Her friend told her not to worry, but to listen as Minst was speaking again.

9

"So Jesus had passed beyond the Station known as 'The Women of Jerusalem' and he was nearly at the top, just by the oak tree, when he fell again. He had been through so much pain. This fall was awful and he collapsed to the ground. While I was there in Jerusalem, I sensed the great pressure of the crowd as they surged around the fallen Jesus. I felt their pleasure in forcing him to that place where he was going to be crucified. The crowd sat down to watch the spectacle."

10

"Just imagine it was all of us villagers who were grouped around the old oak tree on the rise up there. The time had come to strip Jesus of his clothes. I find this Station so tragic. I saw Jesus as the truth. It was not just his clothes that were being stripped off. It was everything that he stood for. I was wracked by a wave of desperation."

11

"Jesus was absolutely naked. His raw flesh was dragged onto the cross beam of wood. They held him down, took really big nails and hammered them, straight through his wrists, into the wood." It was only when Minst described this that the sheer horror of the crucifixion really came home to the villagers.

12

"The next station is called 'He dies on the cross'. If it had been up here, Jesus would have been crying out in agony as we villagers lifted the cross beam up onto that stump of a tree."

The chief priest said that the feet of Jesus would have only just been off the ground.

"True," said Minst, "but it makes no difference if his feet were just off or right off the ground. He was still going to die a horrific, slow, painful death."

13

"The next Station is called, 'He is taken down from the cross.' I must have spent as long looking at this one as I did at any of them. I felt so much for Mary, the mother of Jesus. I'm sure that all the crowd would have drifted away and that it is only at this moment that she was able to touch his body in peace. She was human and Jesus was her son. Yes, I am deeply touched by this part of the story."

14

"She and her friends then took the body and wrapped it up and laid it in the tomb. As it says in the Bible, the stone was then rolled across and the tomb was sealed. I met many people in Jerusalem and for them this was the last station, but not for me. I am sure that we all know the story about just what happened on the first Easter day, how they found the tomb empty and Jesus gone. He had risen and lives on."

15

"So I see one more station, which I call 'The living Lord'.

All those fourteen Stations were there in Jerusalem but this one I have brought home with me."

Here Minst looked slowly and intently around at all the villagers.

"I brought this Station with me when I left Jerusalem, but when I arrived here I found it was already in this village."

There were murmurs of confusion.

"Yes, it is for you and for me. It is for every one of us."

He held out his right arm and slowly he swept it all around, over the villagers, the houses, out over the animals, the fields, the hill and then on around to the people again. He made a complete circle and then rested his hand back onto his chest.

"Here is the fifteenth Station. It is right here in all our lives, whoever we may be. It may sound an extraordinary thing to be saying, but the real lesson that I learnt from travelling my great journey, is that the ones with real wisdom would never go out like that because, what I was seeking, they know is already here with us all in this village."

1

Jesus, a man of truth, is condemned to death by the crowd, through their government.

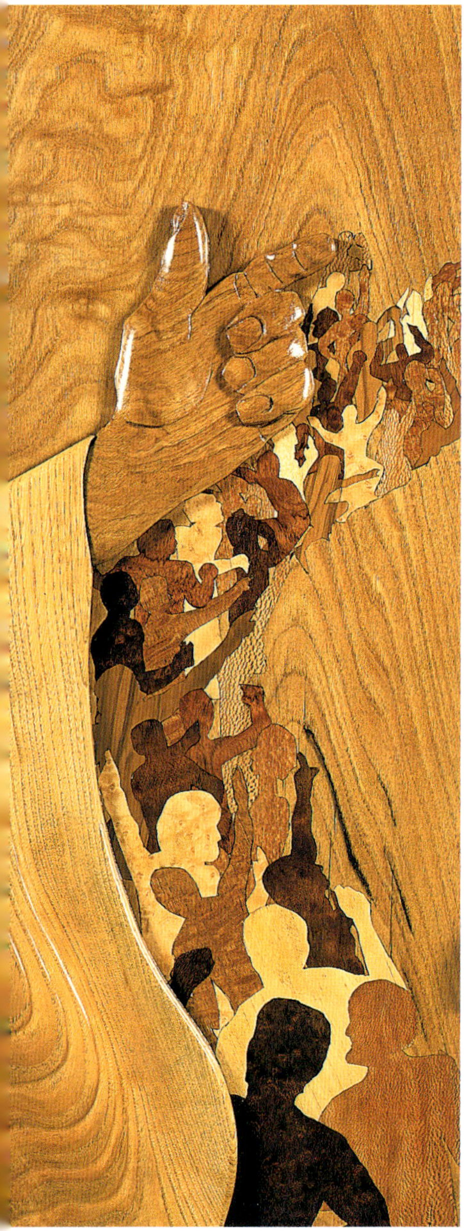

Who is it that is condemning this man of truth to death? It is the government, of course. It is only the government that has such power.

Ah, yes, but in a democracy we are responsible for electing the government and so, even if it is the front for the tricky decisions, we elected the government and so, in this example, we are responsible for condemning the man of truth to death.

But 2000 years ago the crowd was dealing with a dictatorship, so Pontius Pilate had the power. Maybe so, but the people made him change his mind. Who was really making the decisions?

It was the crowd then and it is the crowd today. That crowd includes you and that crowd includes me.

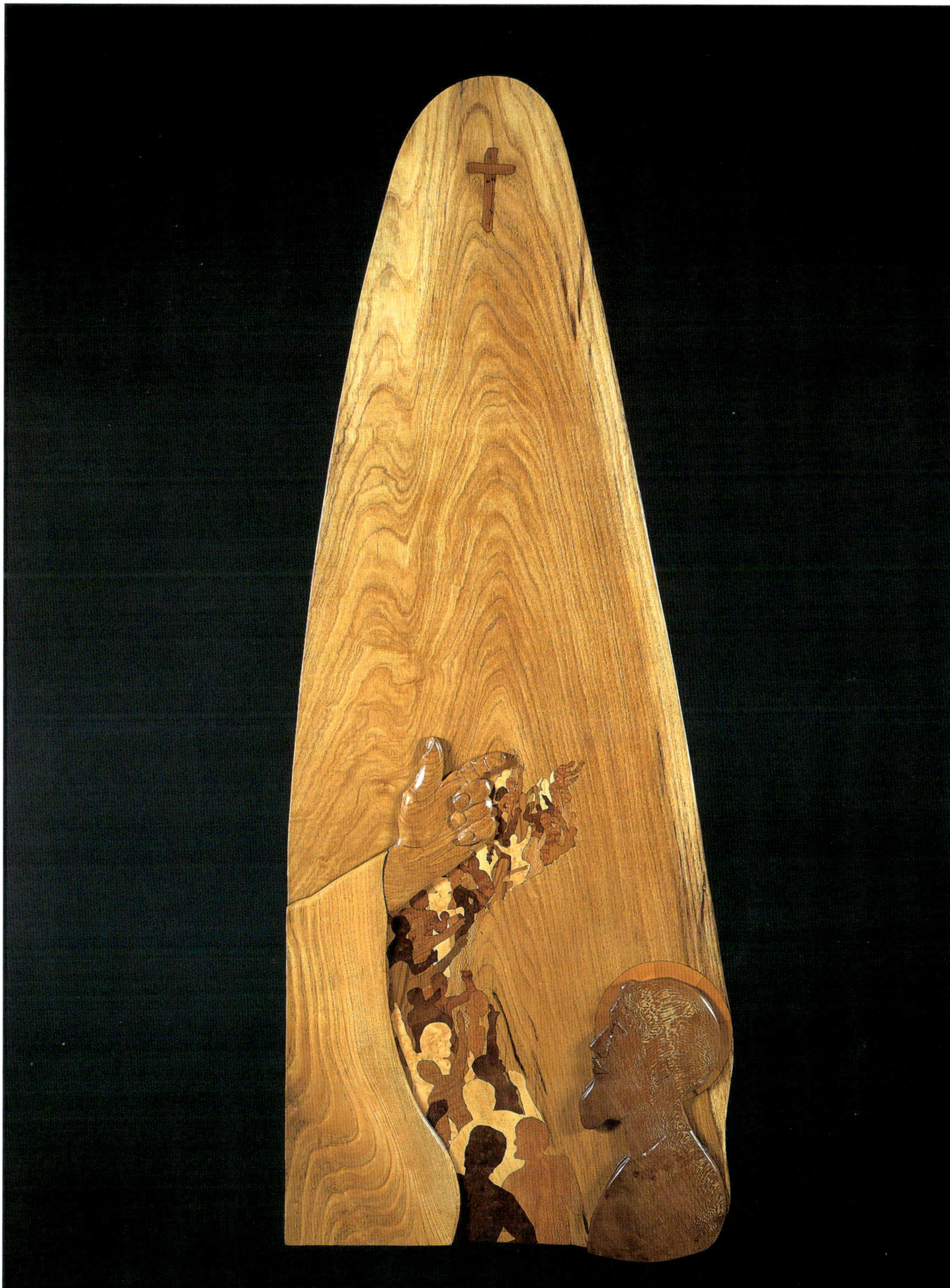

1

2

The truth is beaten and flogged and roped to the execution beam.

There is this energy, a force. The push of the people has been rolling now for some time and has been centred on steering the government into condemning this person to death.

Success now and time for action. No turning back. With every lash a cheer goes up. The waverers cannot stay silent. They are sucked in too. Anybody who does not agree with the action must find a small space, right at the back of the crowd, just for their own safety. But these people are included in the view of the crowd and the crowd is large.

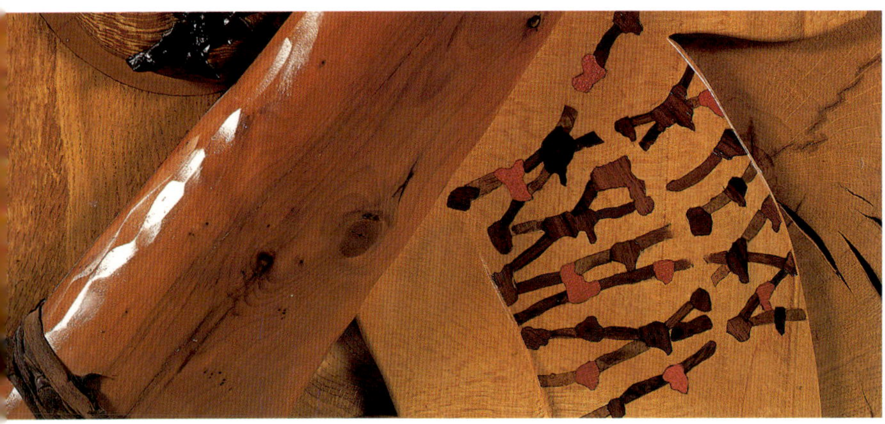

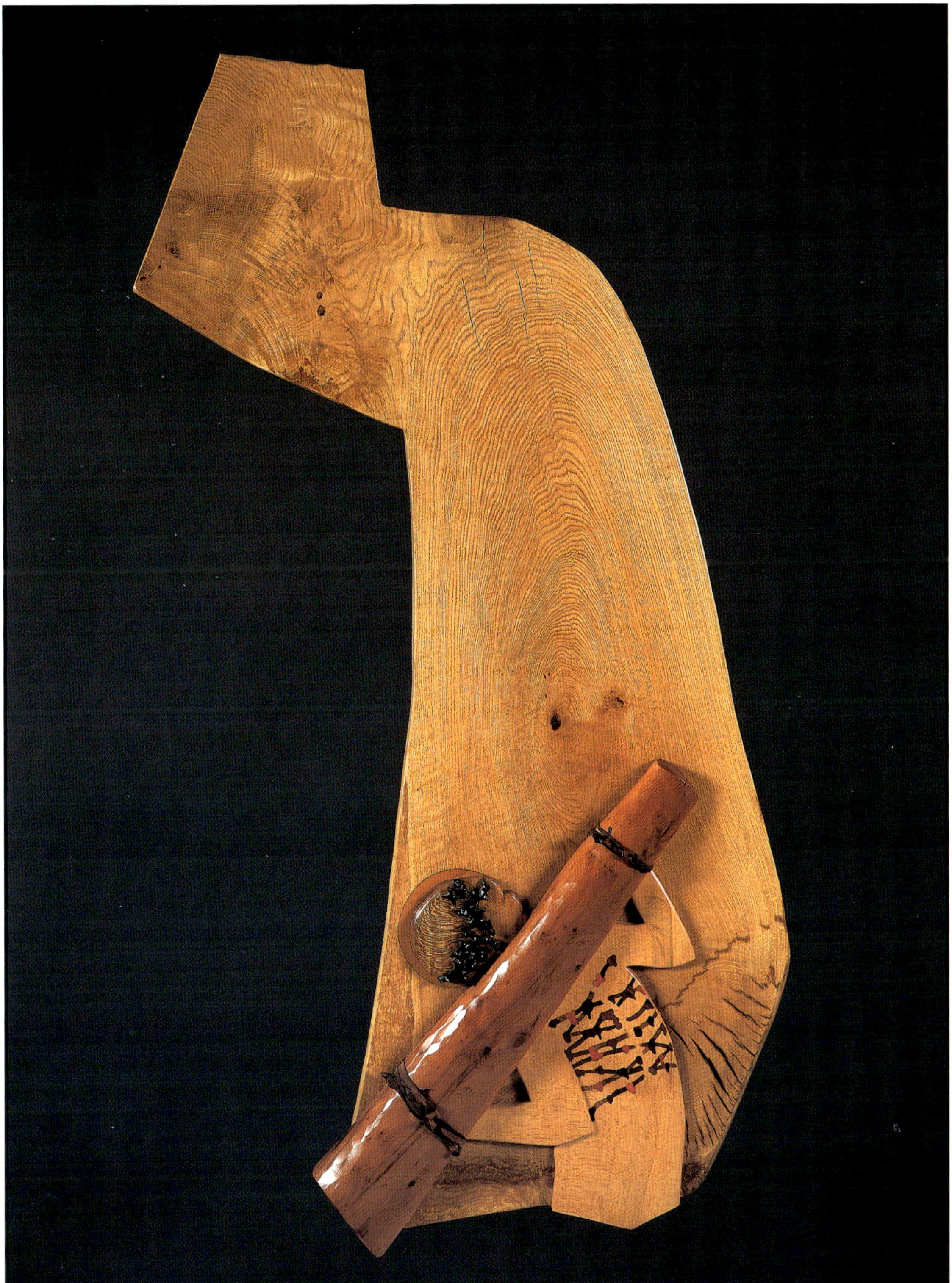

2

3

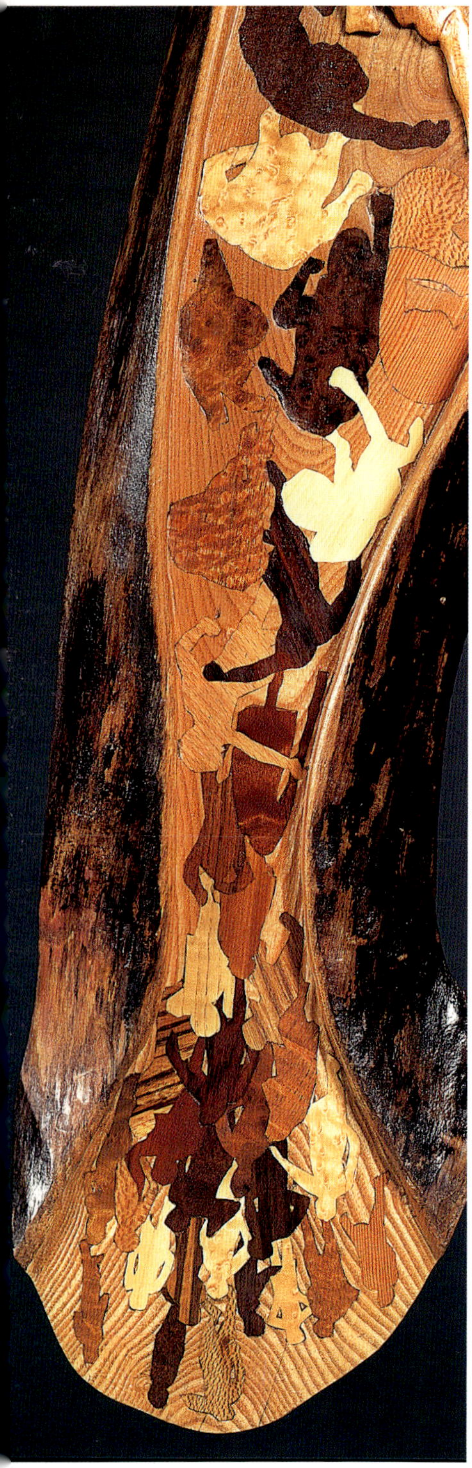

He falls under pressure from without.

You push, he falls. You are directly and solely responsible.

This is pressure that we can control. We are not being forced into this position by anybody else, even if they are telling us to do it. Traditionally soldiers with spears appear in this station. Those soldiers come from our community, they are paid from our taxes and they are governed by our government.

We are responsible for our own actions as he falls under pressure from without.

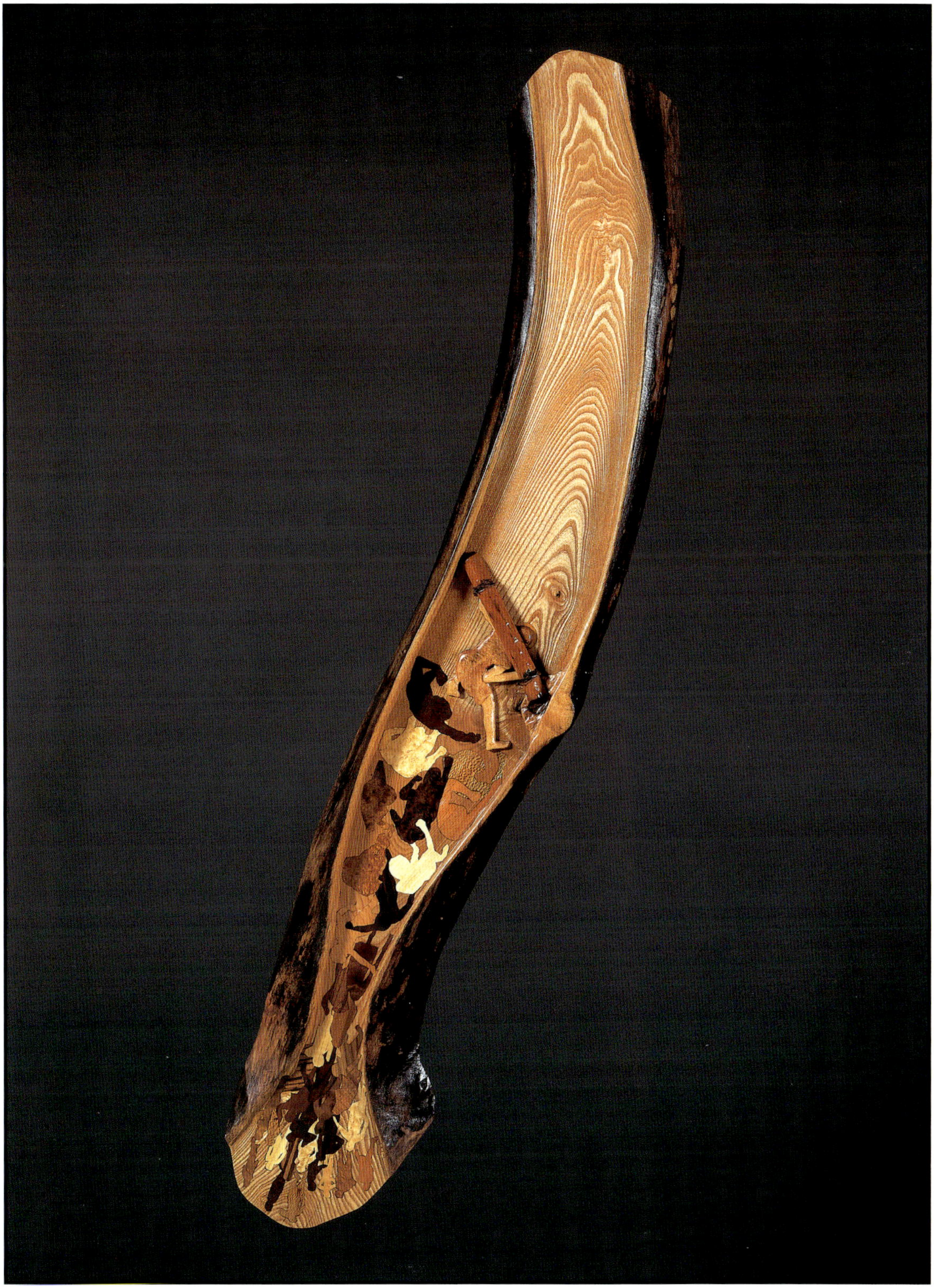

3

4

He is helped by his mother.

A moment of supreme compassion. Compassion from within his family. She, his mother, is there at the side of the path. She reaches up to her son. A moment of supreme communication. Their eyes meet, they are one, their hands hold and energy flows.

To the followers of Jesus he is the supreme man. To the followers of Mary, she is the supreme woman. To many she represents Mother Earth.

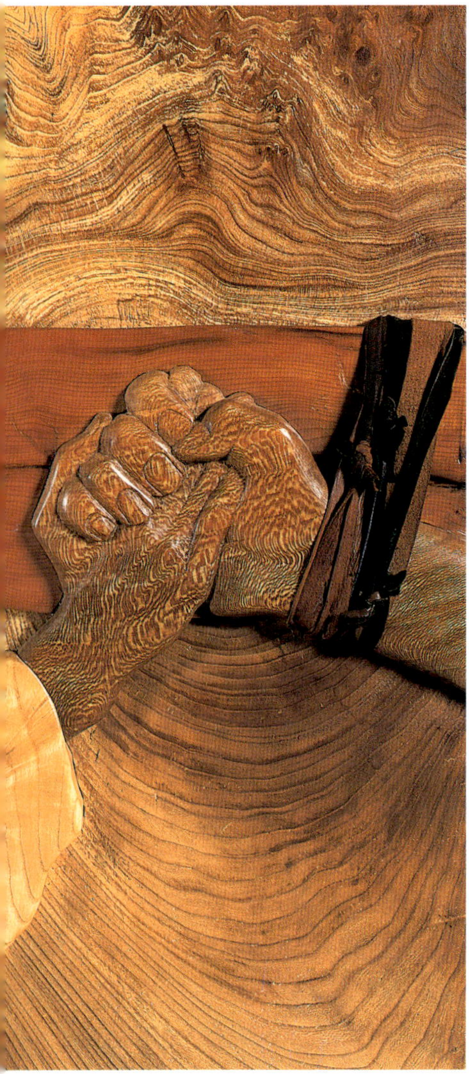

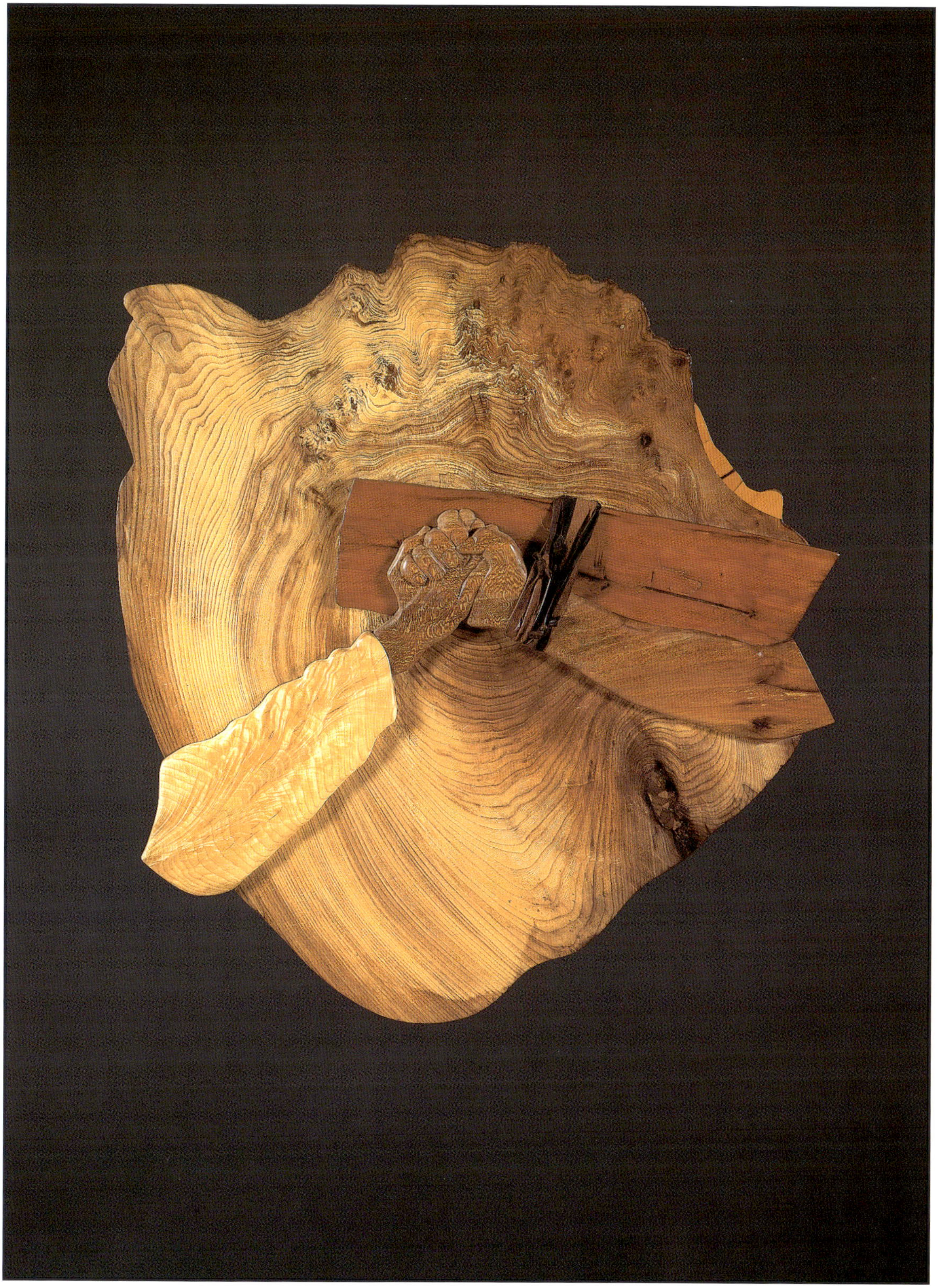

5

He is helped by Simon of Cyrene.

The noise, the screaming, the howling. The crowd has only to move the truth to the execution ground.

Oh no… all is not right… he has been beaten too hard. But here is a friend of Jesus. They could see it in Simon's eyes. Come on then, help your friend, you help him with the weight of that beam of wood.

So Simon comes out of the crowd and puts his arm around Jesus. He puts his arm around the man he loves.

The essential sympathy of Simon speaks to us all as we relate to each other and as we relate to nature in its extraordinary diversity.

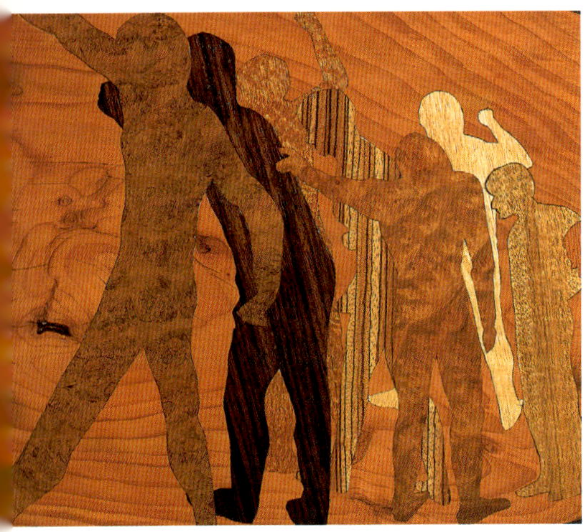

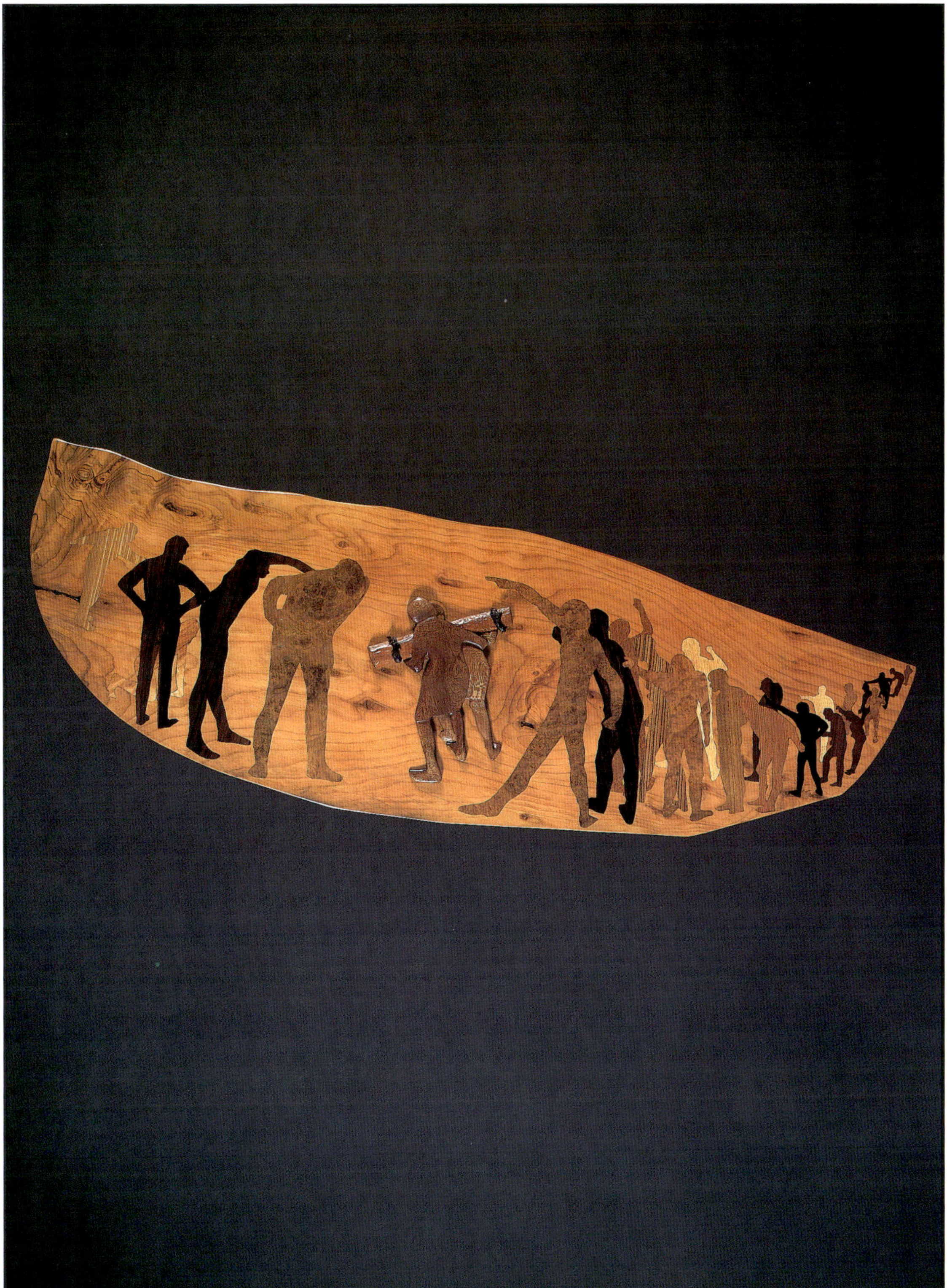

6

He is helped by Veronica, who wipes his face.

The stranger approaches. She is young and surrounded by an aura of compassion.

Vero means true and Icon means likeness. Veronica, Vero icon, the true likeness, the image left on the cloth. The face of the very essential truth that is in all of us. So, my face is there on the cloth, your face is there on the cloth and indeed Veronica's own face is there on the cloth.

To some this is a carving showing the unity of all people that live in the world. To others it goes much further.

It is showing the essential centre
of every sentient being
and on
to all plants and the substance of the earth
and out
to the limits of the universe.

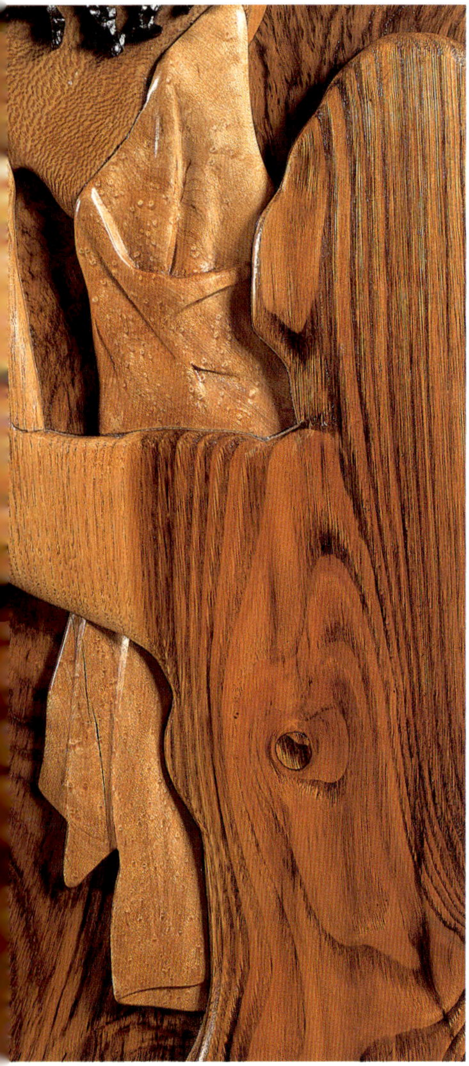

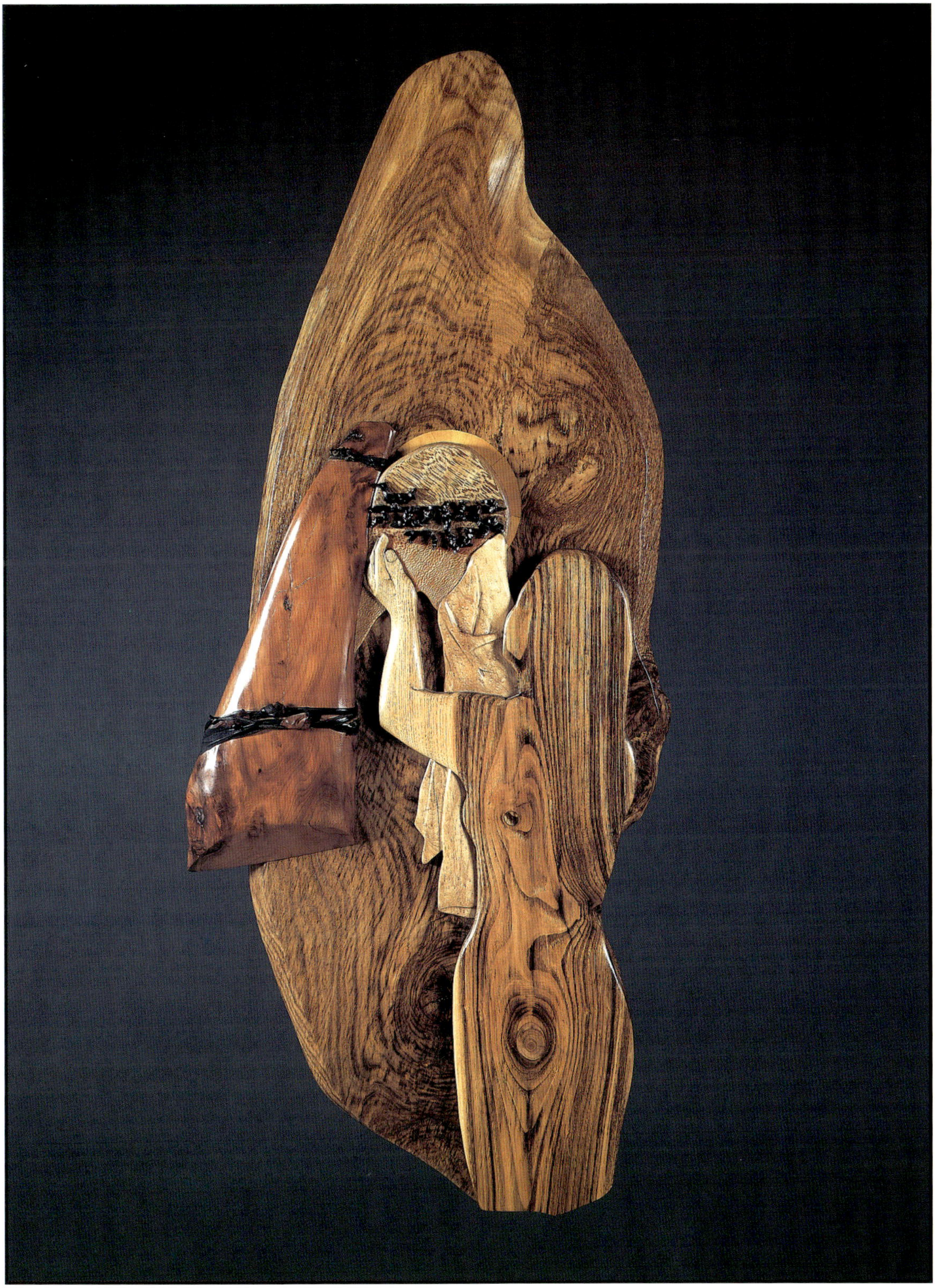

7

He falls for the second time under pressure from within.

Pressure from within can have so much more force than pressure from without because this pressure may be there every hour of the day and every hour of the night.

Desire, aspiration, ambition.

We do have some control over these pressures that we feel coming from within ourselves.

When the crowd in our mind's eye say 'Go!', then we go. When the crowd in our mind's eye say 'Stop!', then we stop. When the crowd in our mind's eye are in confusion then we are confused.

We can change this state within ourselves. He fell for the second time under pressure from within.

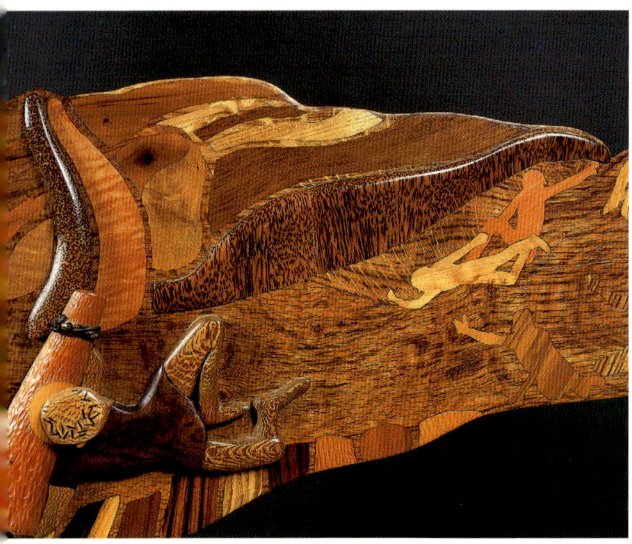

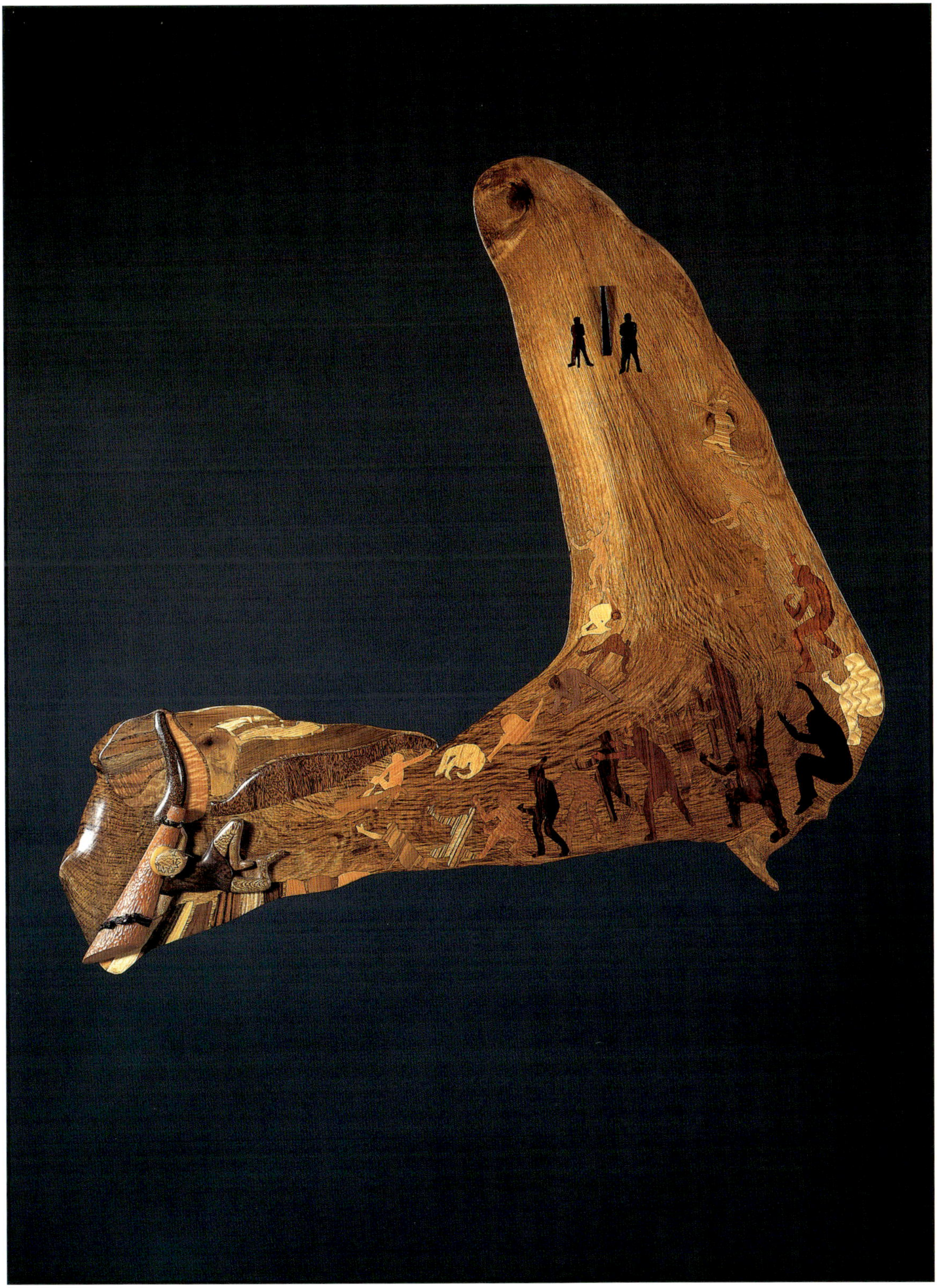

7

8

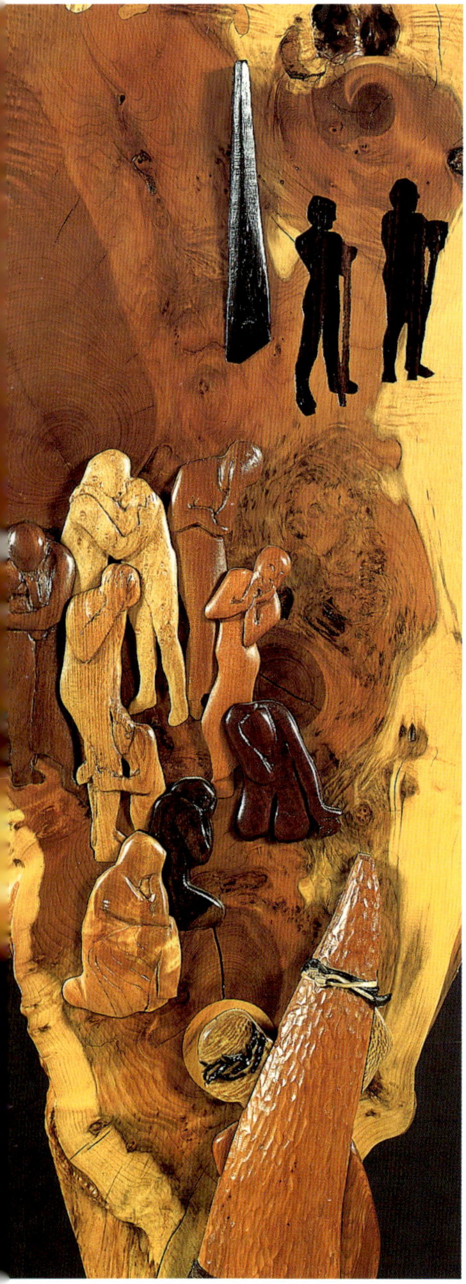

Jesus turning said, "Daughters of Jerusalem, weep not for me but weep for yourselves and for your children. A day is coming when they will say, blessed are the barren and the wombs that never bore and the breasts that never gave suck. Then they will begin to say to the mountains 'fall on us' and hills 'cover us'. If they do these things when the tree is green then what will happen when the tree is brown?"

Luke 23

This is a future statement.
To one it means this and to another it means that but it is a future statement.

We are all building the path that leads to the future. If we choose to build the path with a twist in it, then the future must twist that way.

Hey come on, relax! I hear you saying that you are not driving this train. 'Please go away while I enjoy my coffee.'

'Yes and please don't hassle me either. I am not even on the train. I have my own car!'

If this happens when the tree is still green then what will happen when the tree is dried up?

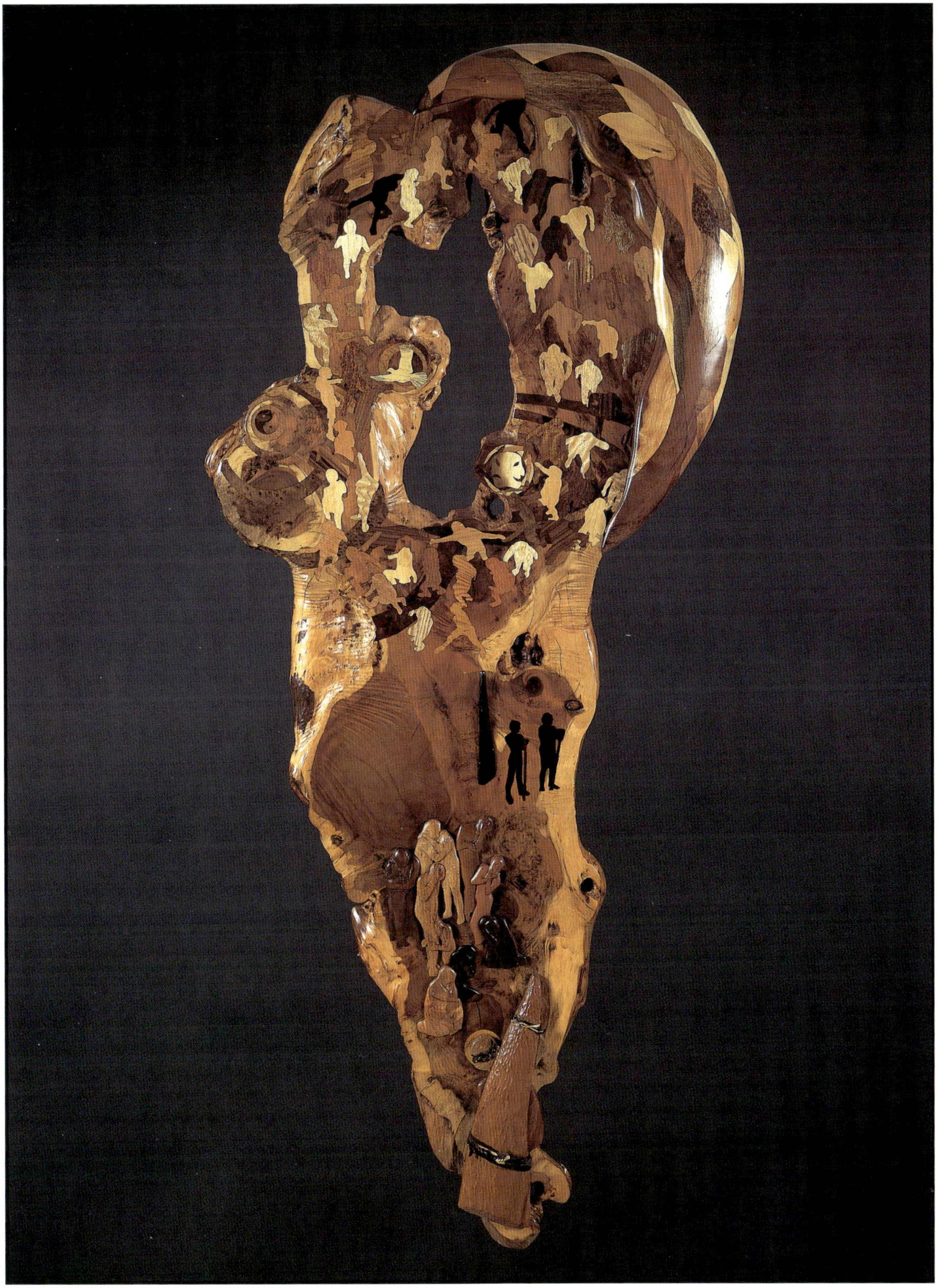

8

9

Under great pressure from the crowd he falls for the third time.

There may be no sound, one's eyes may be shut, there is no particular smell... but the pressure is quite intolerable.

It might be the wind suddenly blowing a curtain that causes the breakdown, the crash, the third and final fall.

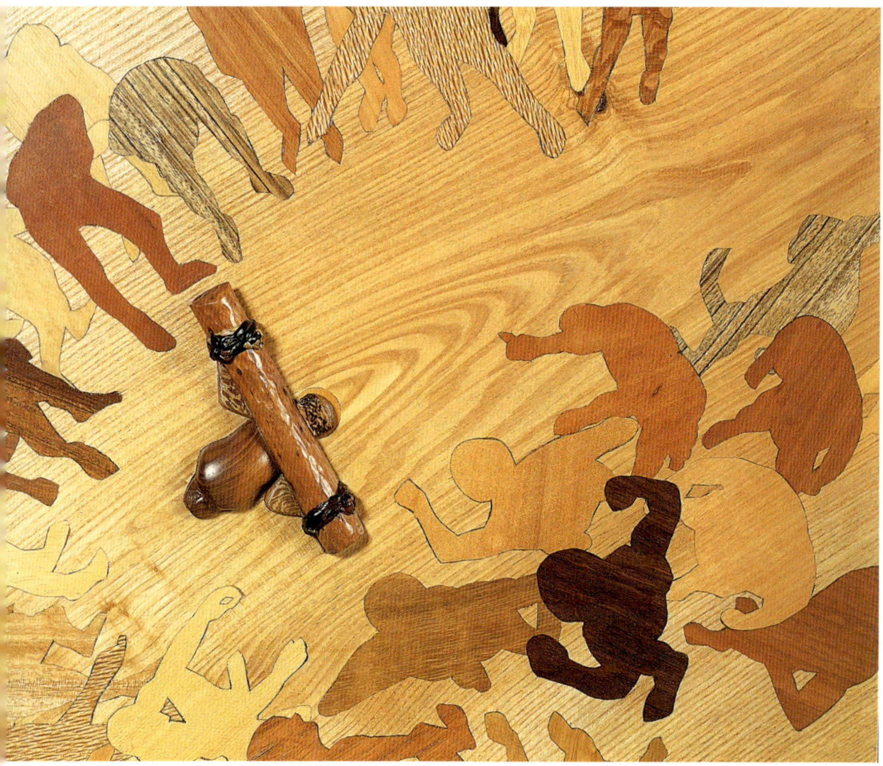

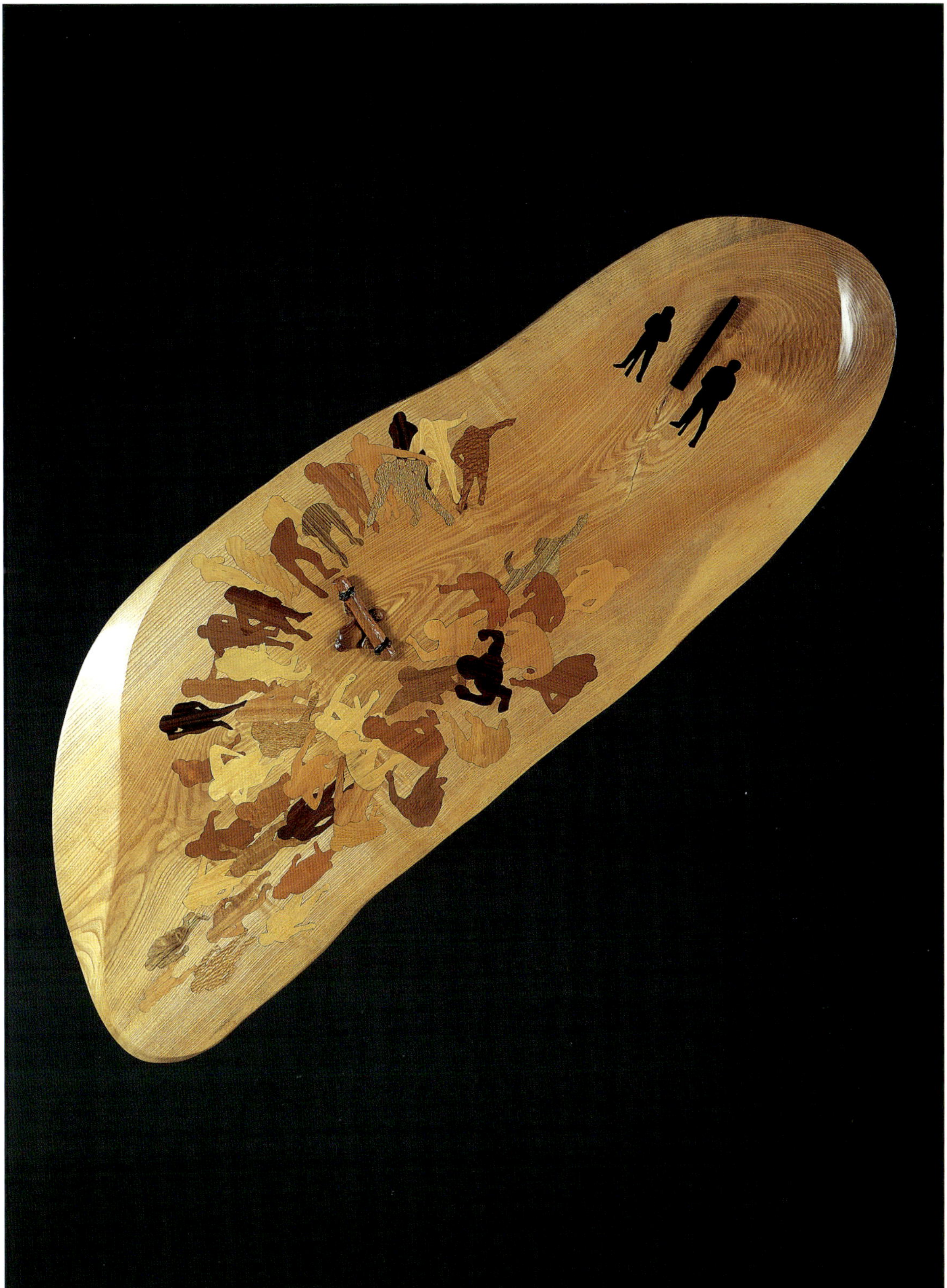

9

10

We strip him of his clothes.

A moment alone.
A moment between torture in life and torture of dying by crucifixion.
A moment of supreme awareness.
A moment of one between the body, the immediate surroundings and the universe.

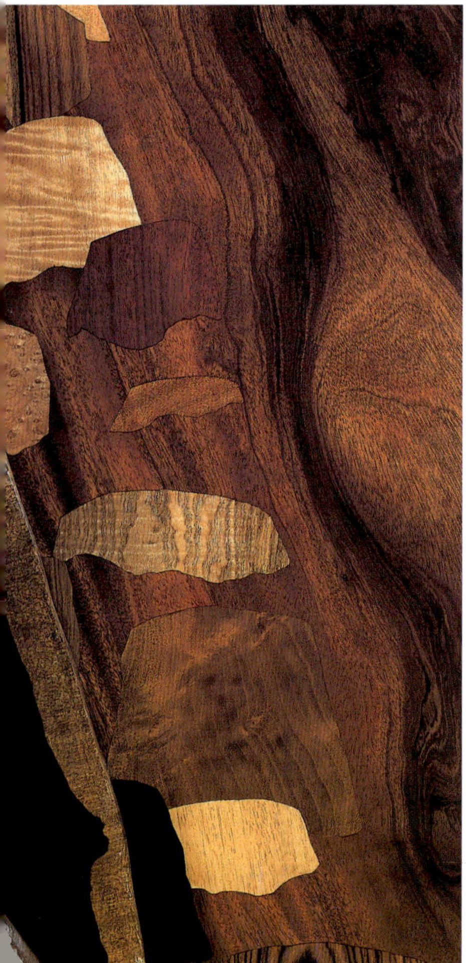

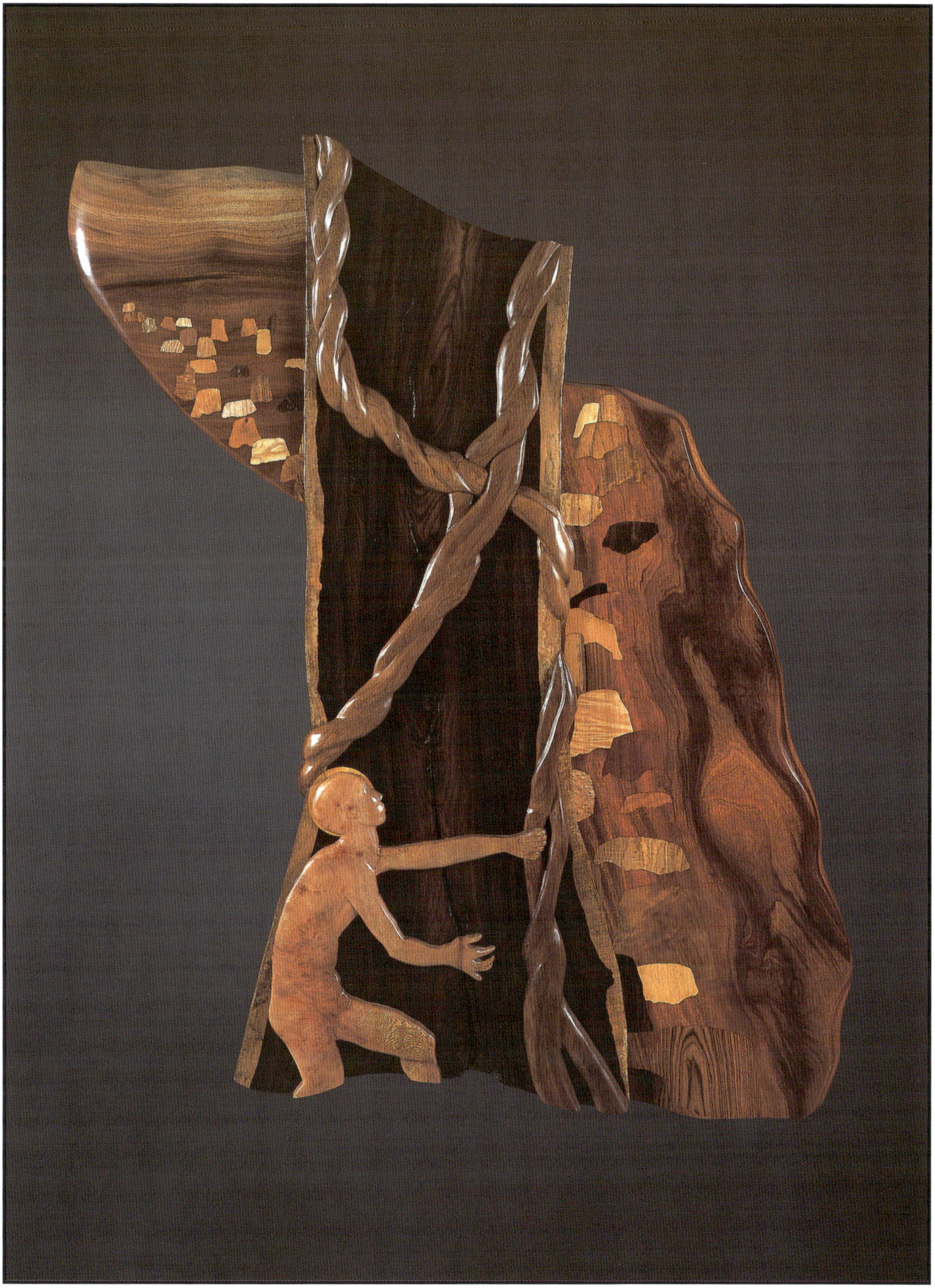

10

11

Jesus is held down by the crowd as the tools of government drive in the nails.

It may be by the government. It may be by their forces.

But there is no point from which we can avoid responsibility if the truth is sacrificed.

We employ the government.

The government employs the force.

The force drives in the nails.

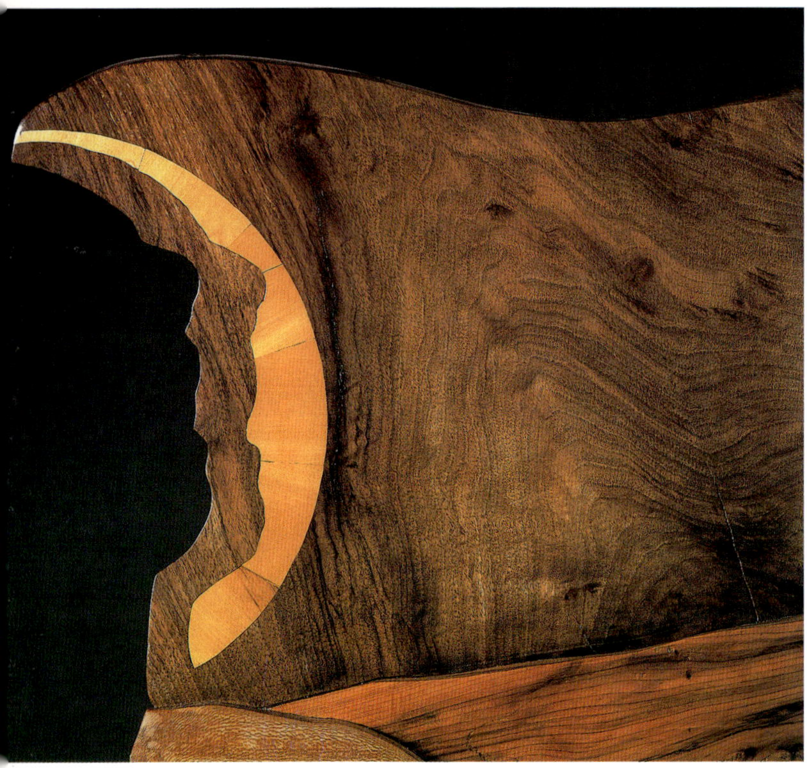

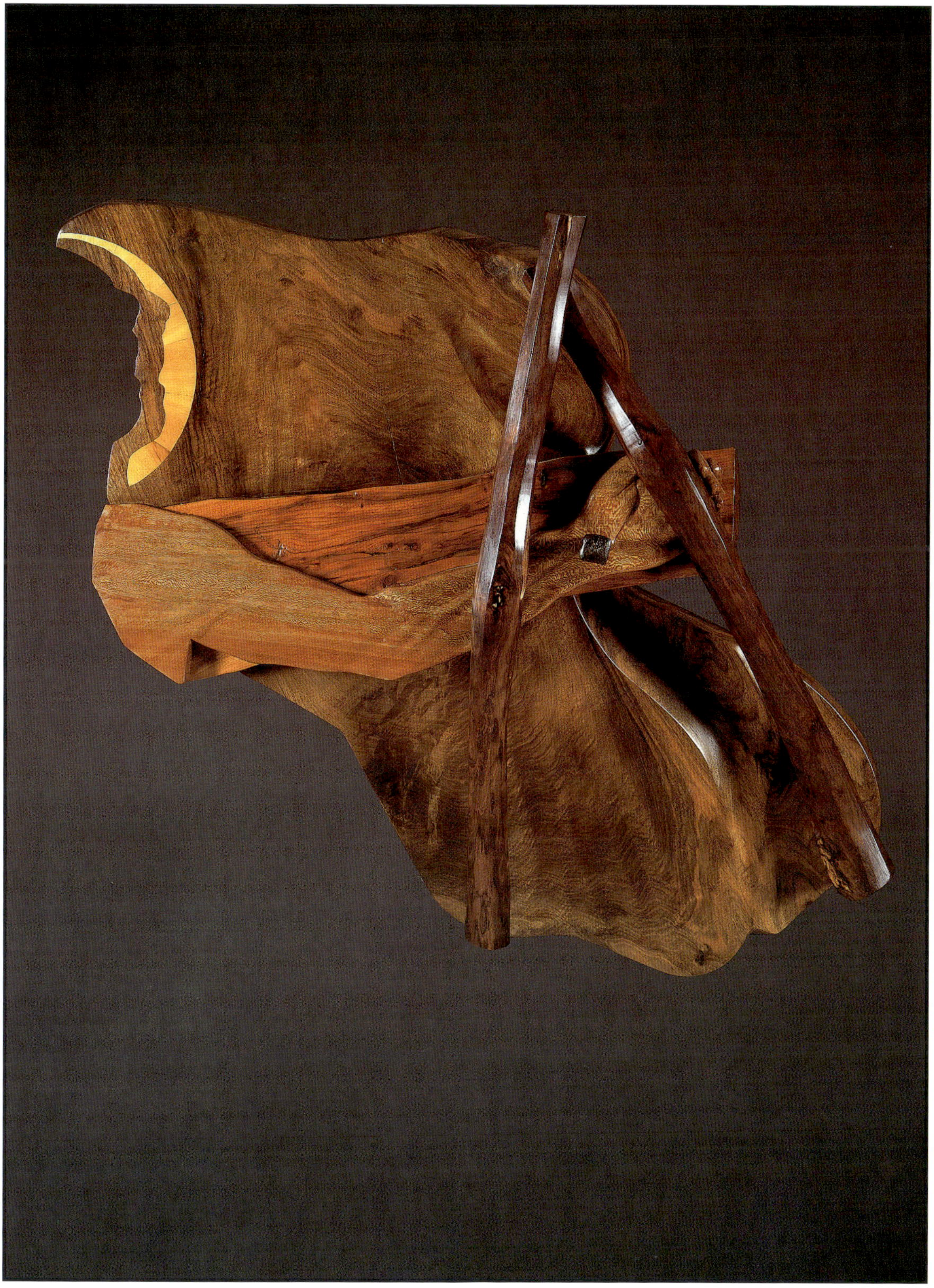

12

He is executed on the cross.

There is no need for great
celebration.
It appears to be a fact.
Mission accomplished.
But a factor has been ignored.
So sorry, the job is done.
Yes, I have watched it. The truth
has been crucified.

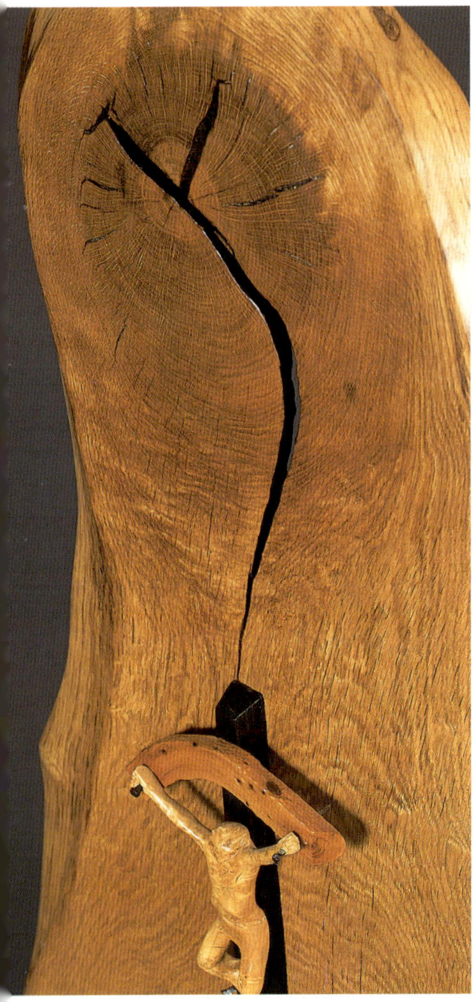

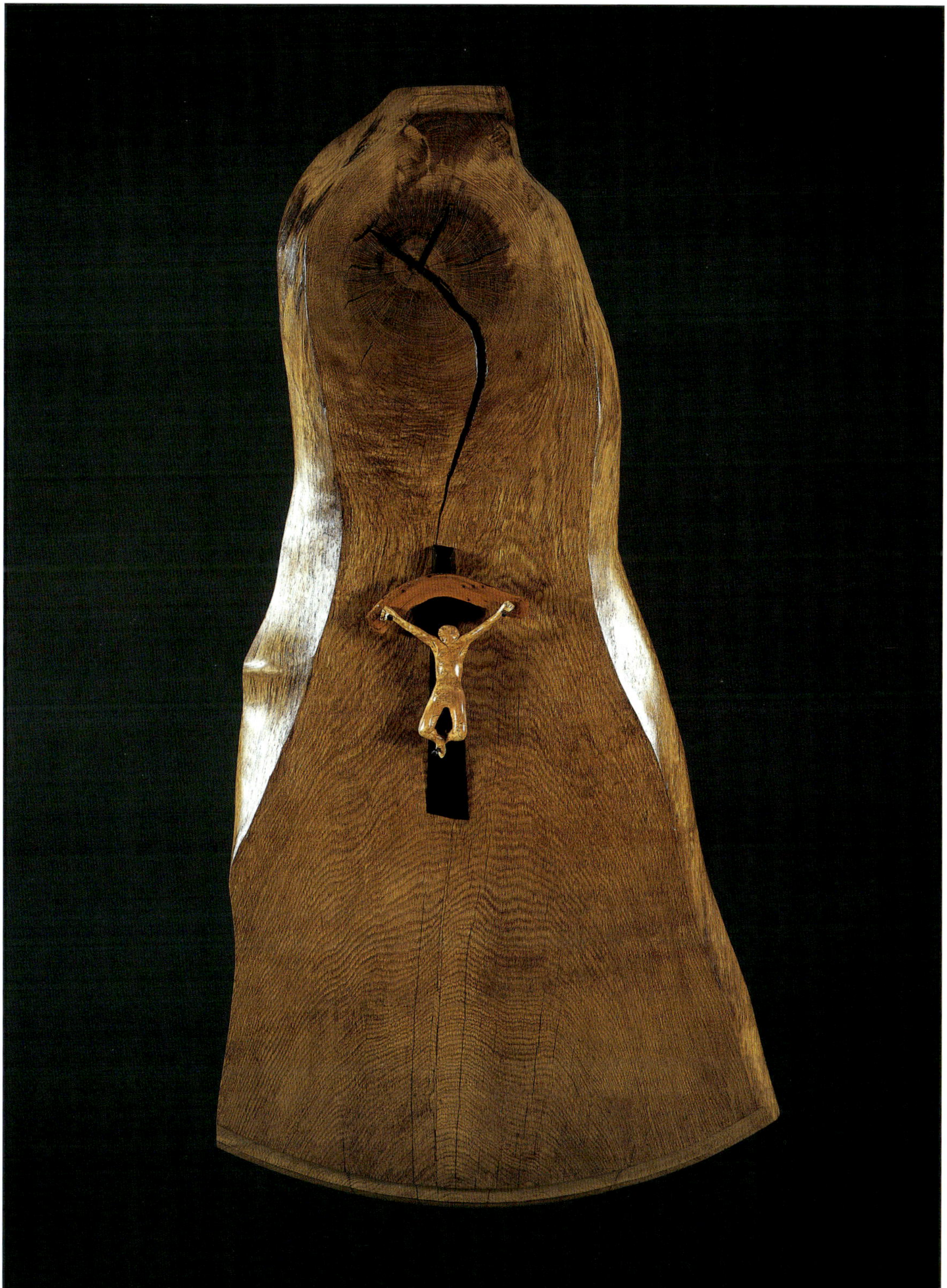

13

The body of Jesus is held by his mother.

She felt the fact.
  She was the fact.
  She held his body in her arms.
  The mother gives.
  The earth receives the body
back unto herself.

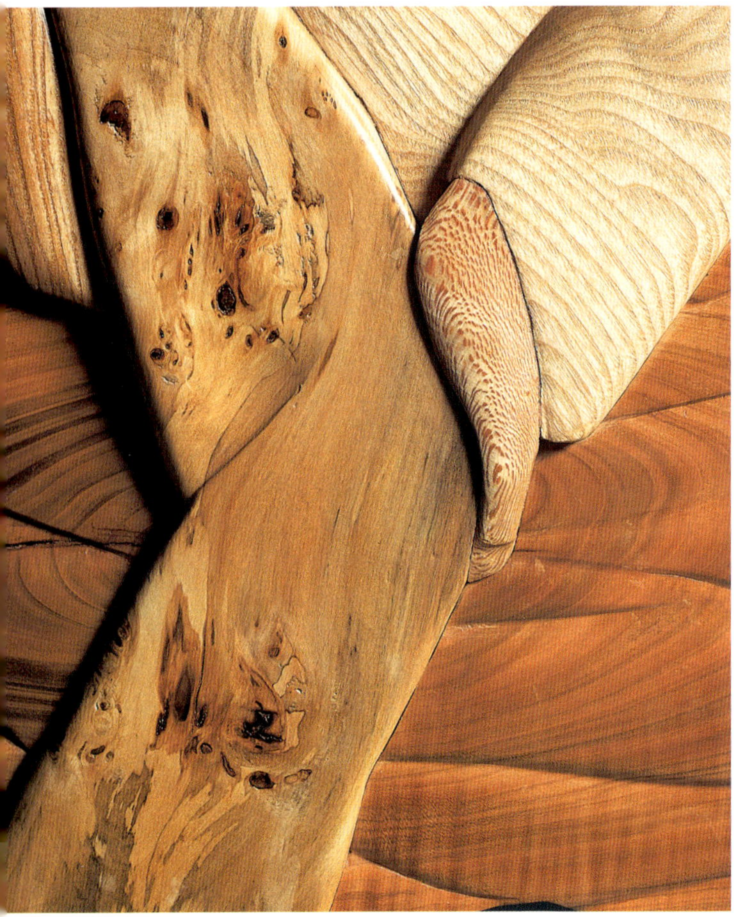

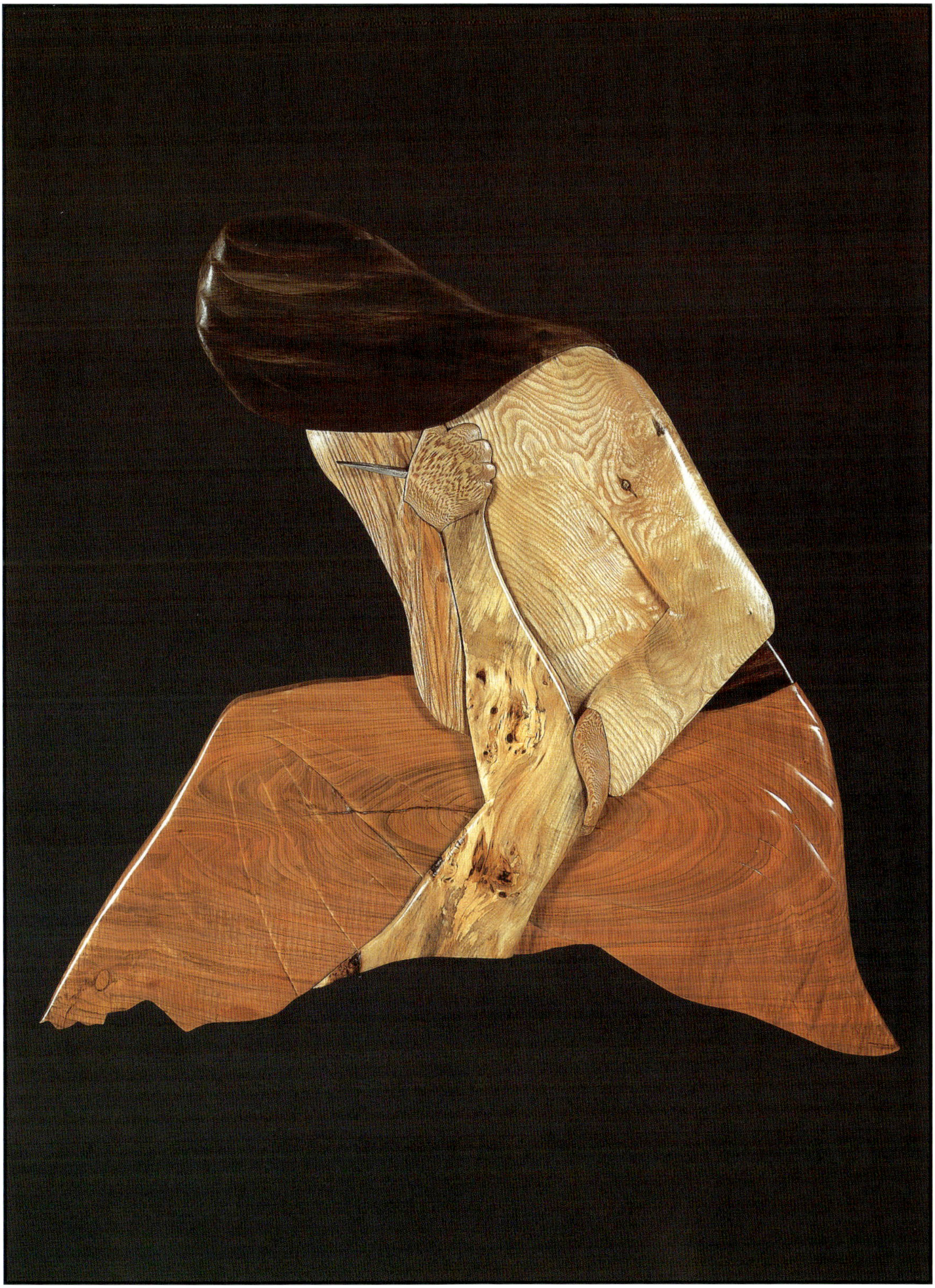

14

He is enclosed into his tomb.

It appears that the body grows
smaller and smaller,
changes and disappears.
See it.
Smell it.
Hear it.
Sense it.

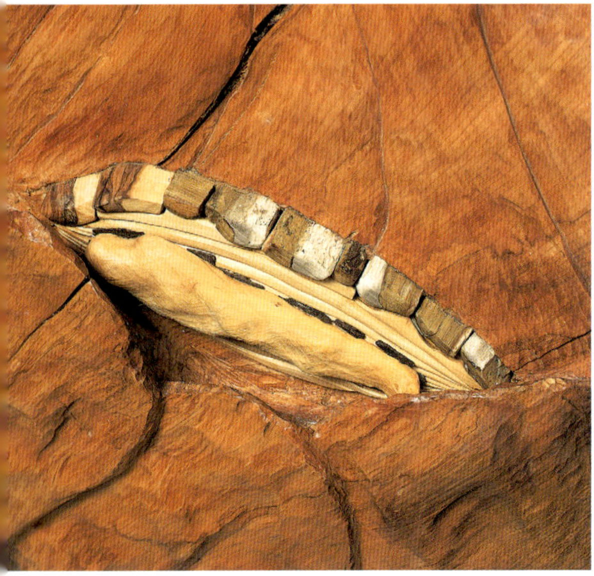

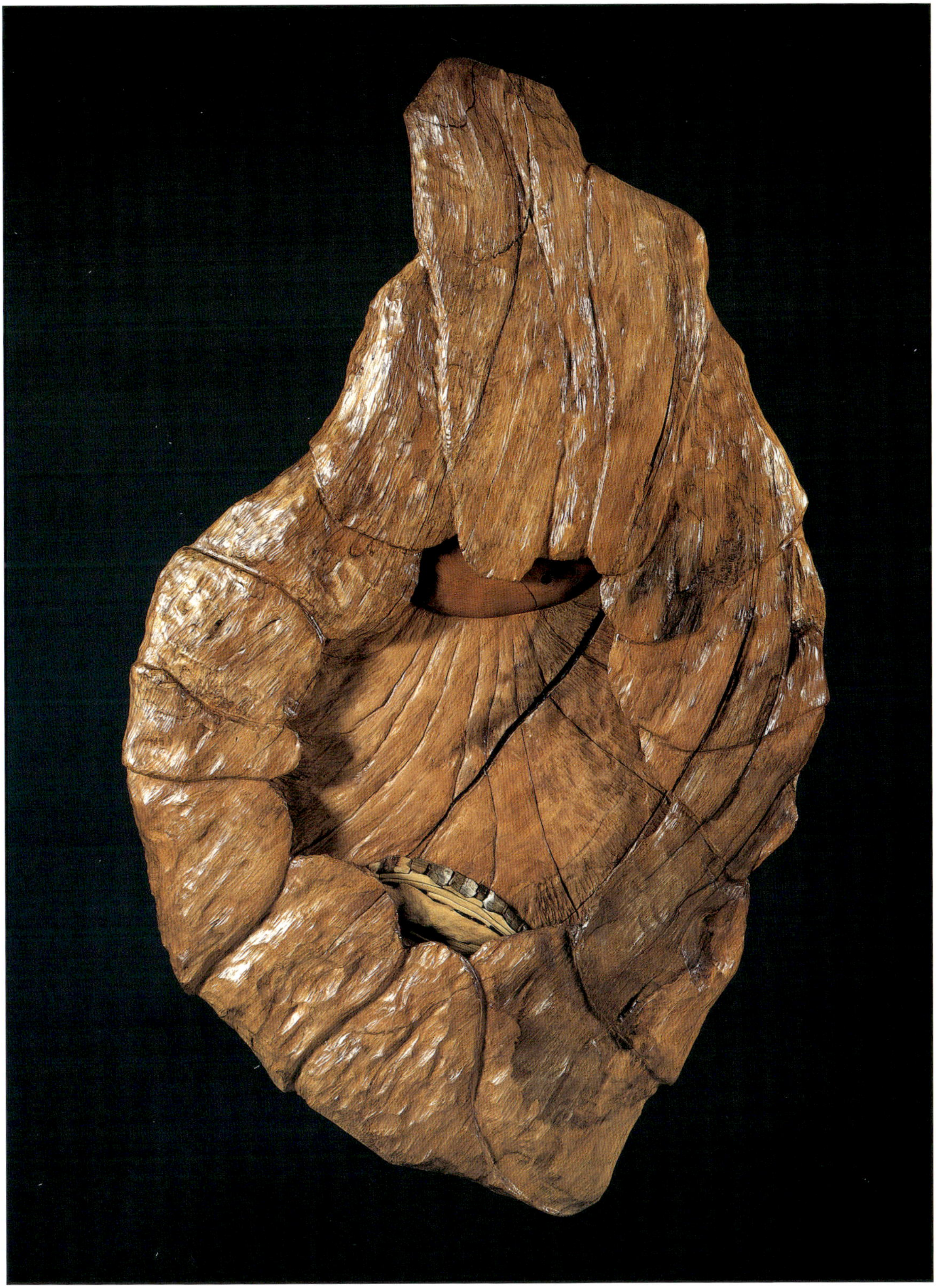

14

15

ILLUMINATION*
****Awareness, Enlightenment, Insight, Inspiration, Understanding.***

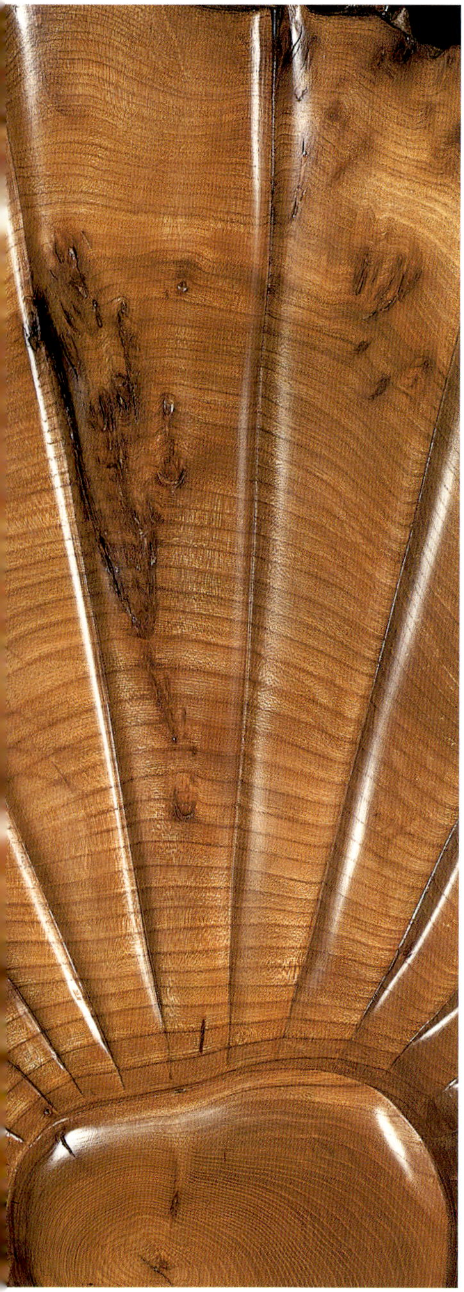

Sacrificing the truth. All that energy.
  So bizarre.
  The truth lived on 2000 years ago.
  It lives today. As does the crowd.
  Look for awareness in enlightenment,
insight into inspiration,
and understanding of
ILLUMINATION.

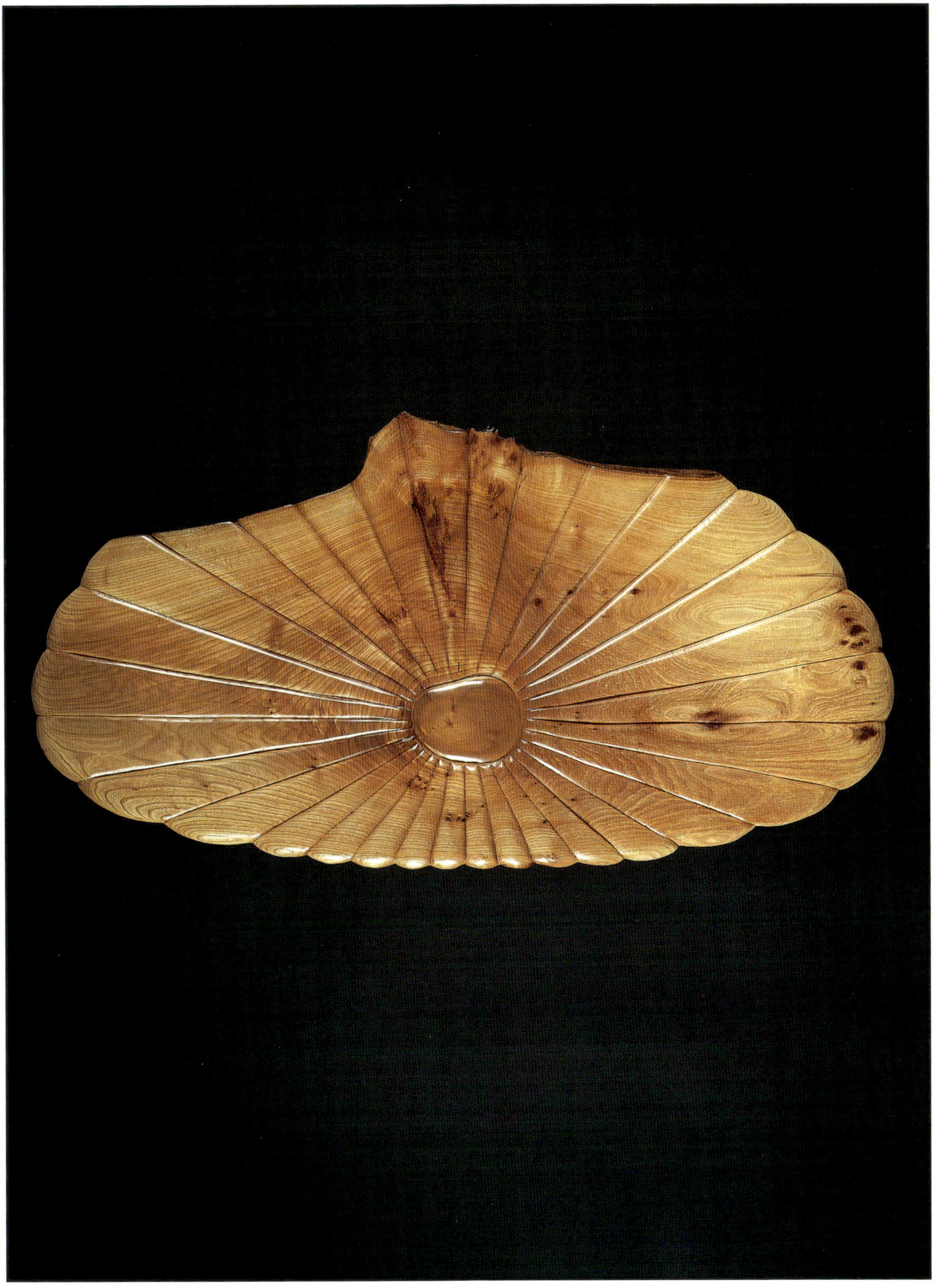

Technical Section

part 1: Veneer inlay method

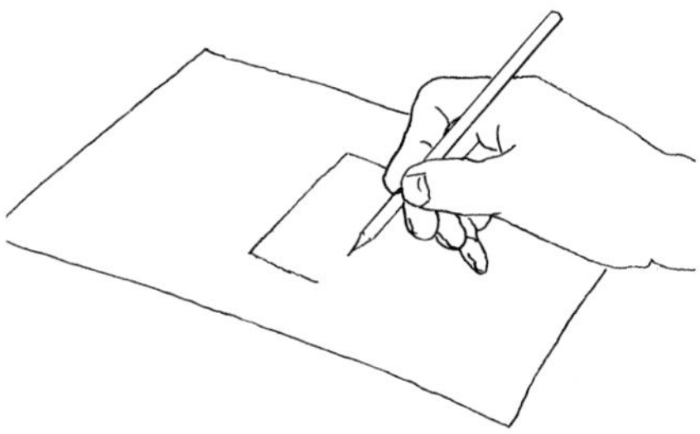

1. Create original art work. In the Forest Stations this usually comes from a drawing or a photograph.

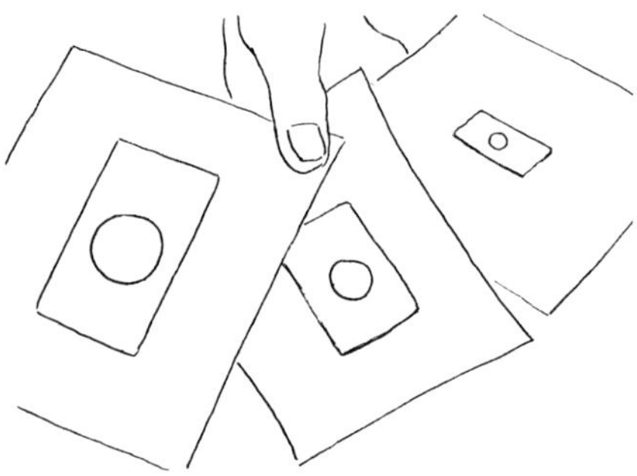

2. Enlarge or shrink the image on a photocopy machine.

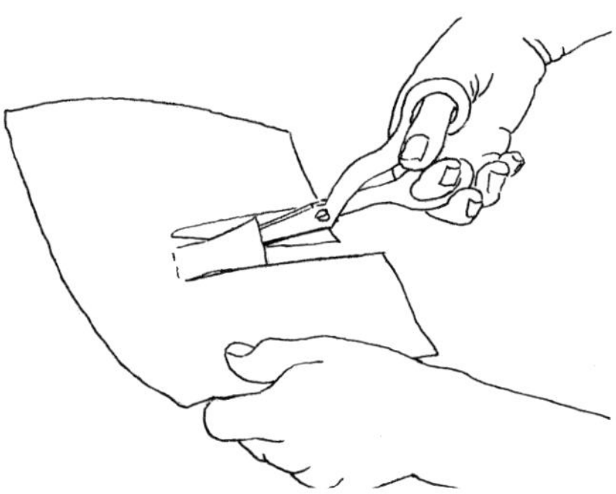

3. Cut out the image with a modelling knife or scissors.

4. Lay the paper onto a veneer and draw around it.

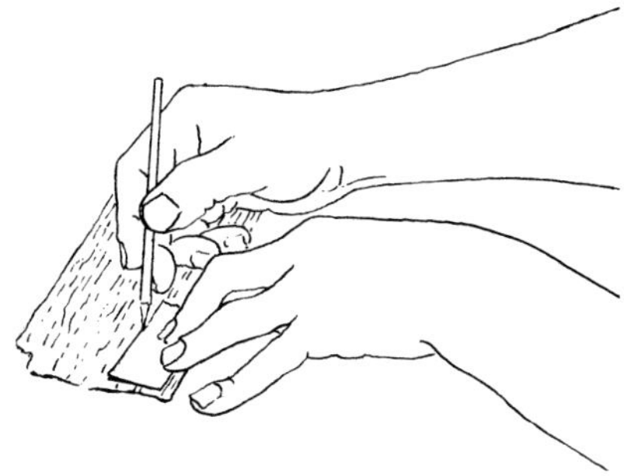

5. Stick sellotape onto the veneer over the top of the pencil drawing.

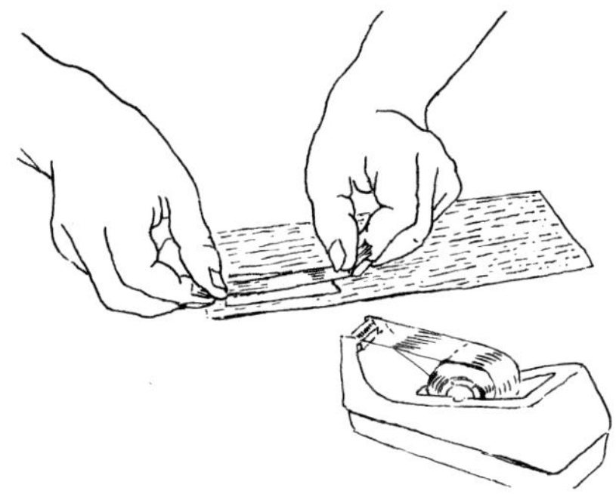

6. Cut out the veneer with a modelling knife.

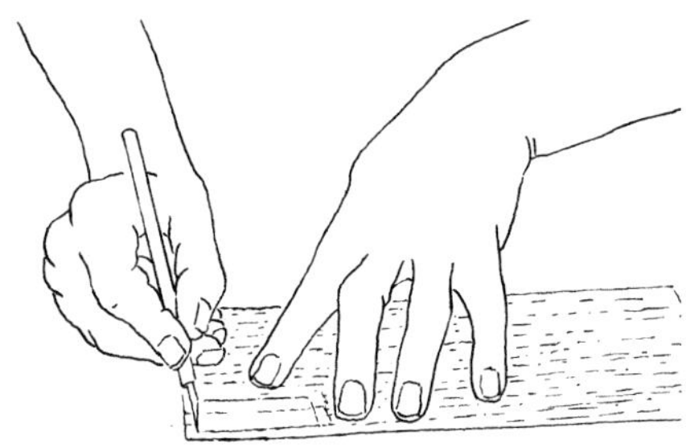

7. Hold the veneer down onto the chosen position on the background timber and draw around it with a 2H pencil.

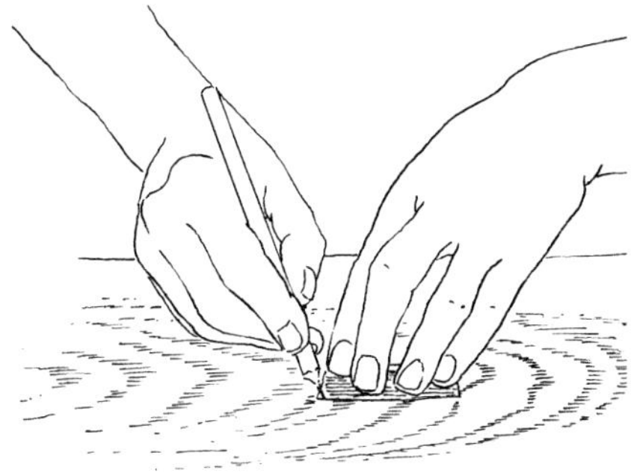

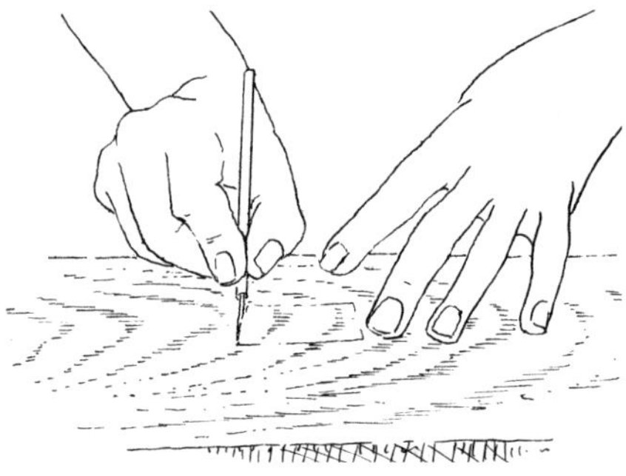

8. Follow around the line with two passes of the modelling knife. The first is soft and creates the path for the second cut which is done with pressure.

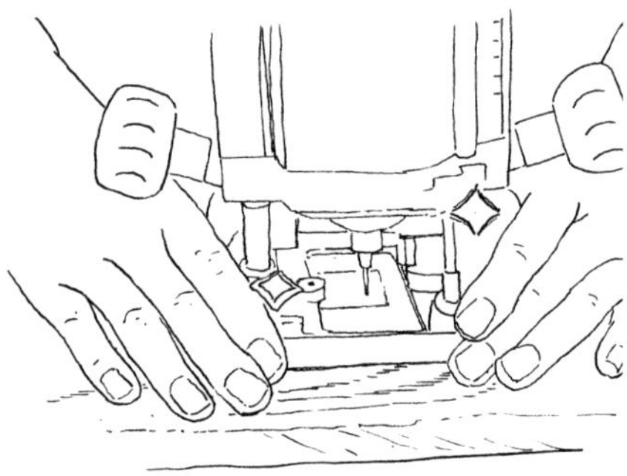

9. Set router to the thickness of the veneer and then rout out the space for the veneer.

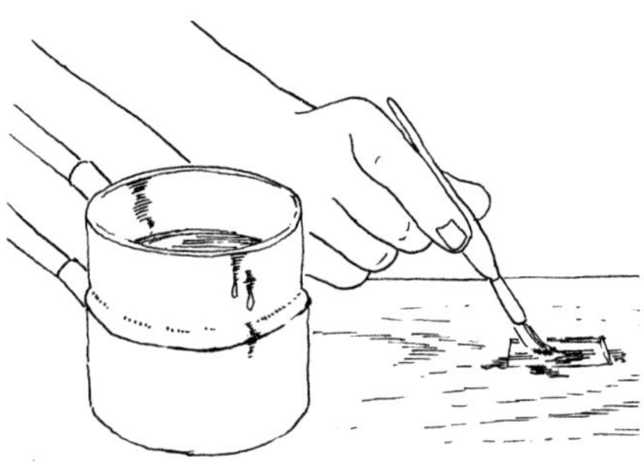

10. Paint scotch glue into the prepared hole. The glue dries immediately.

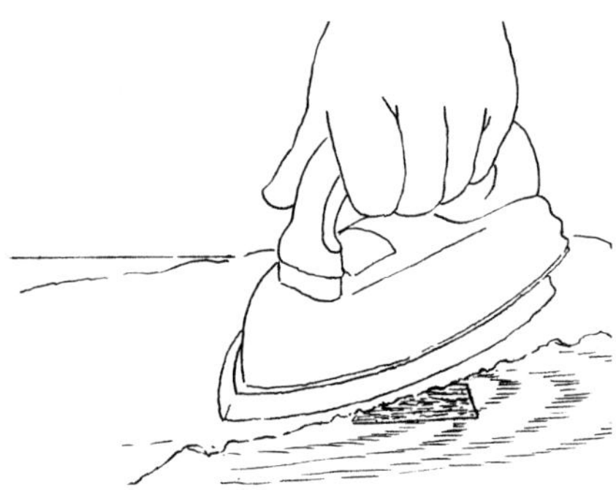

11. Lay veneer onto the glue. Lay felt on top of the veneer and then put a hot iron onto the felt. This will remelt the glue. The heat passes through the felt and the veneer.

12. Immediately take the felt away and roll the veneer flat with a lino roller. This can be done with a veneer hammer but the roller works much better with delicate figures.

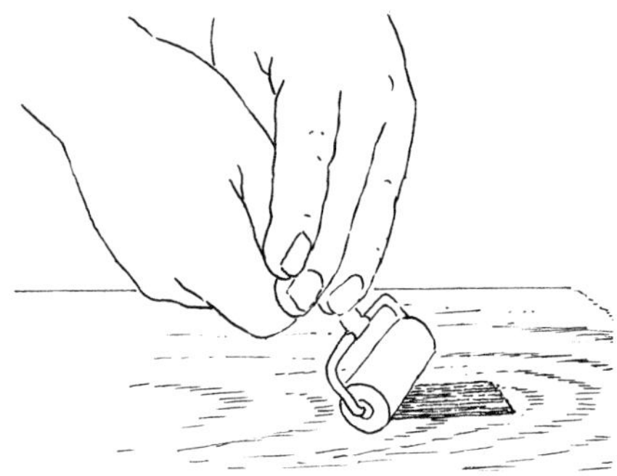

13. Wipe off glue and remove sellotape with a rag which is repeatedly dipped into boiling water.

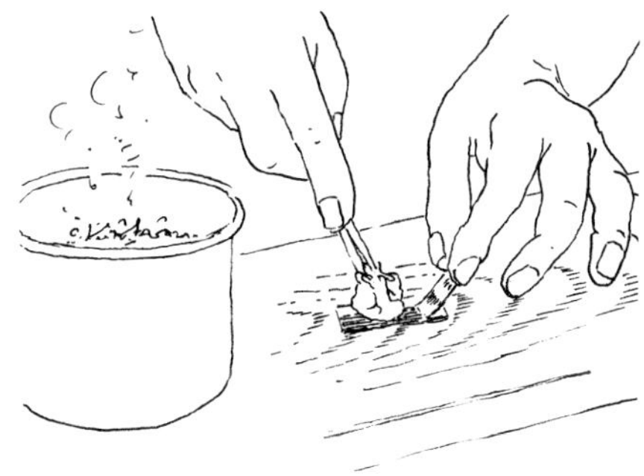

14. To flatten the veneer I either use a cabinet scraper or sand paper on a block. Be very careful here because the veneers are only 0.6 mm thick!

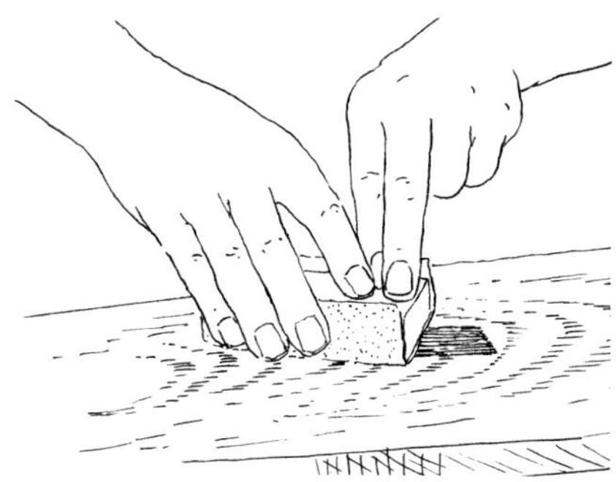

15. Oil, varnish, polish or wax.

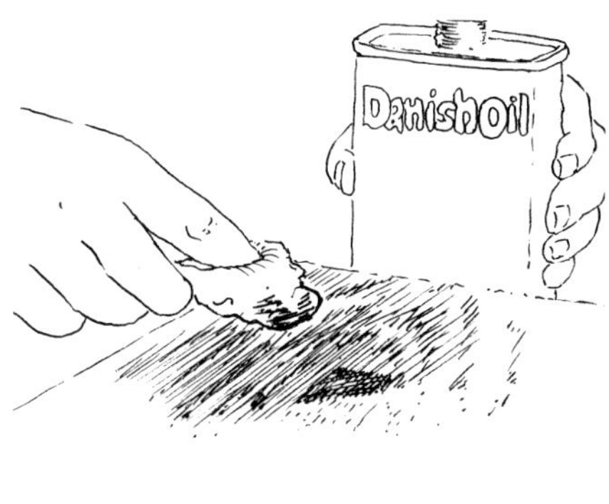

part 2: Identification of all the woods used in The Forest Stations

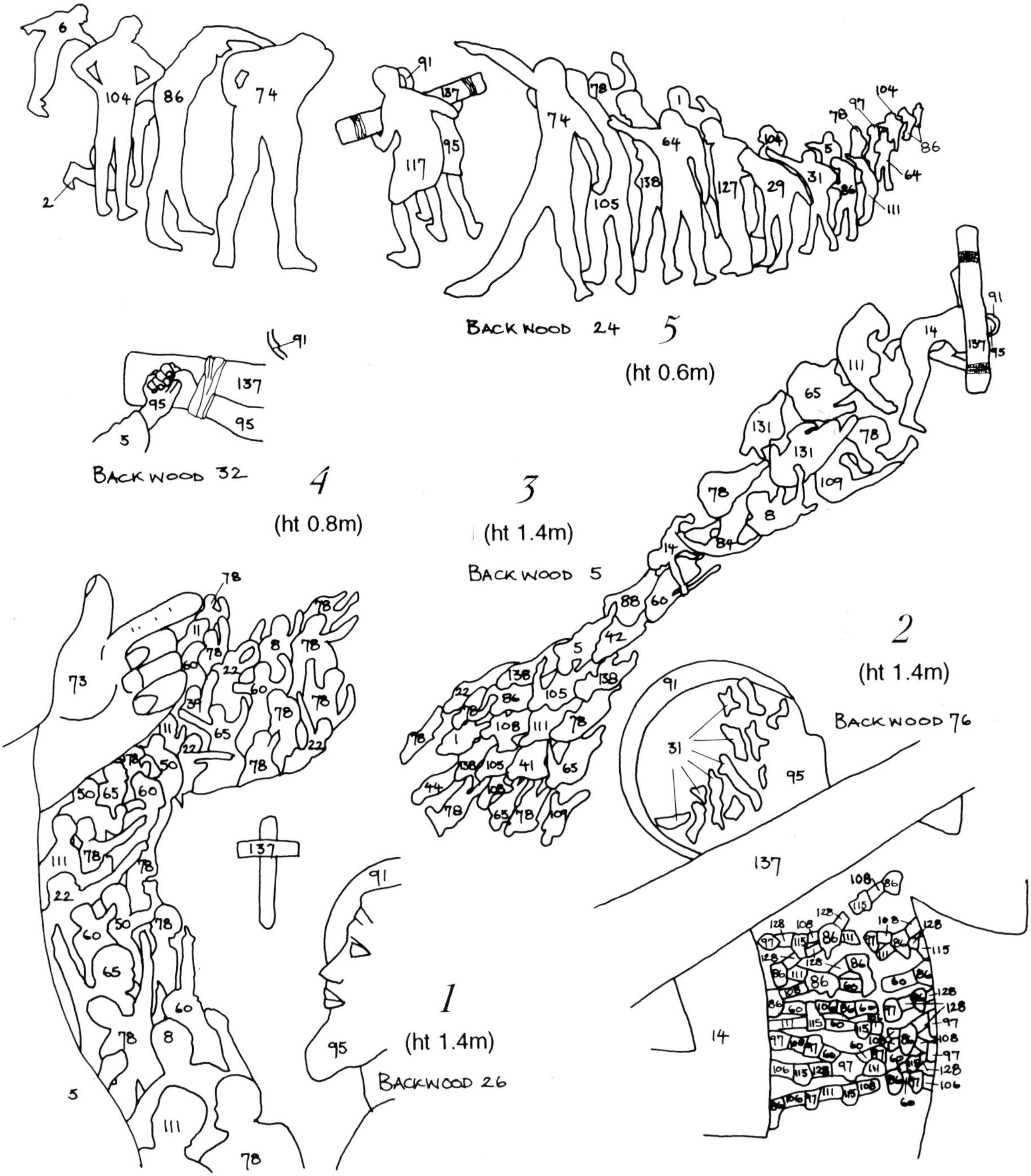

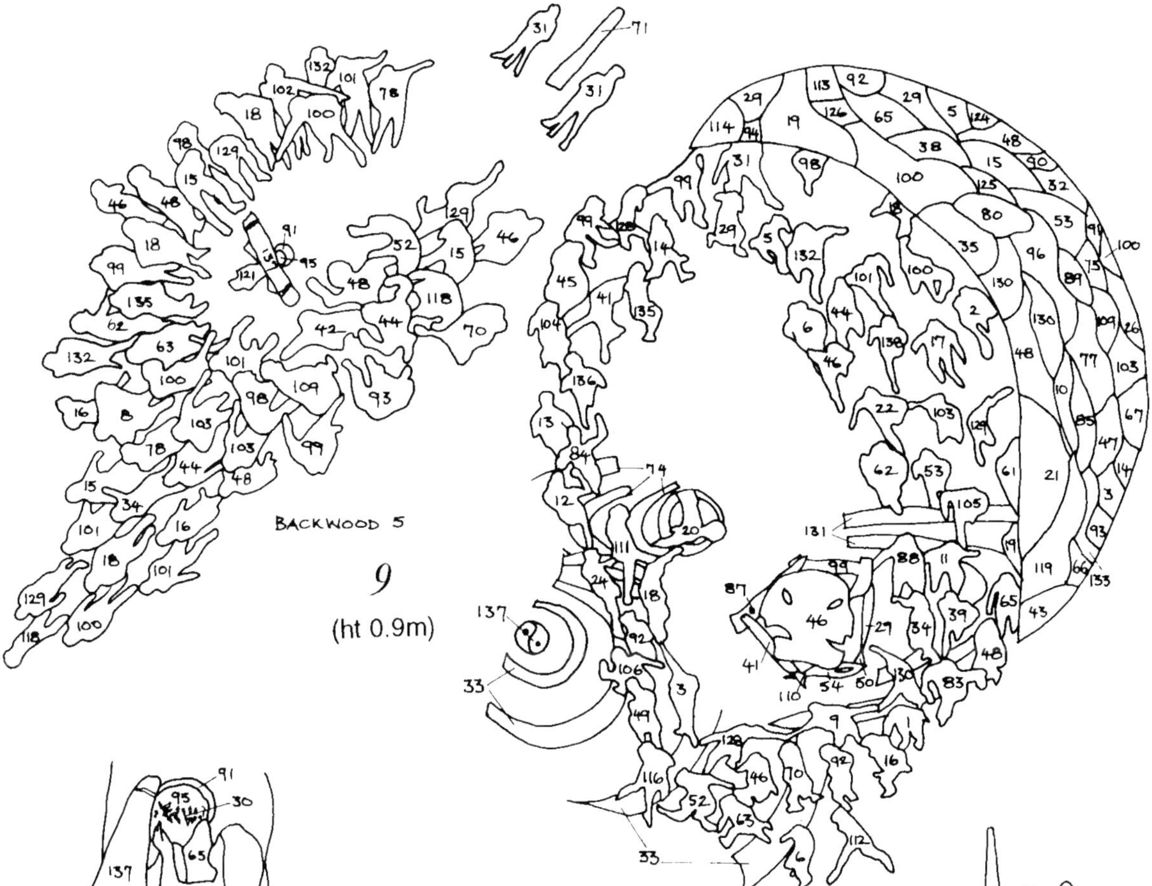

BACKWOOD 5

9

(ht 0.9m)

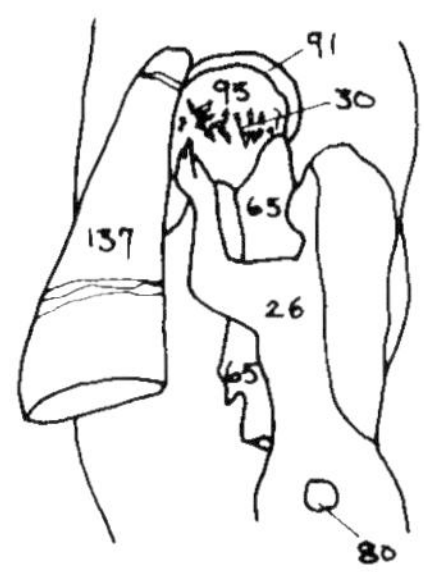

BACKWOOD 79

6

(ht 1.2m)

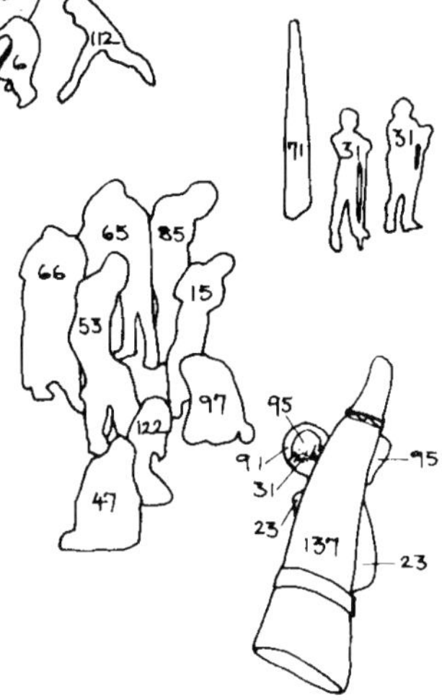

BACKWOOD 137

8

(ht 1.6m)

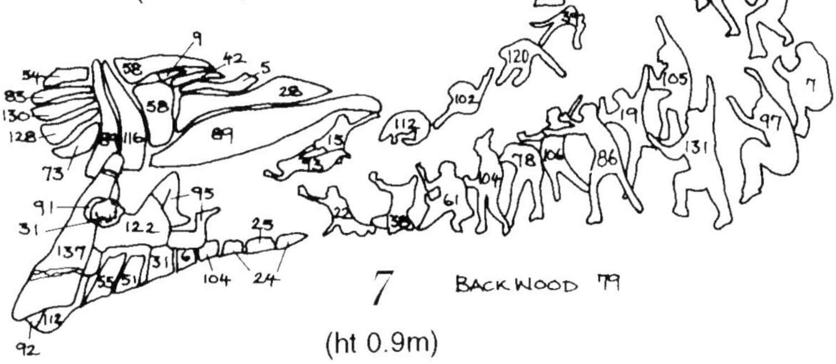

7 BACKWOOD 79

(ht 0.9m)

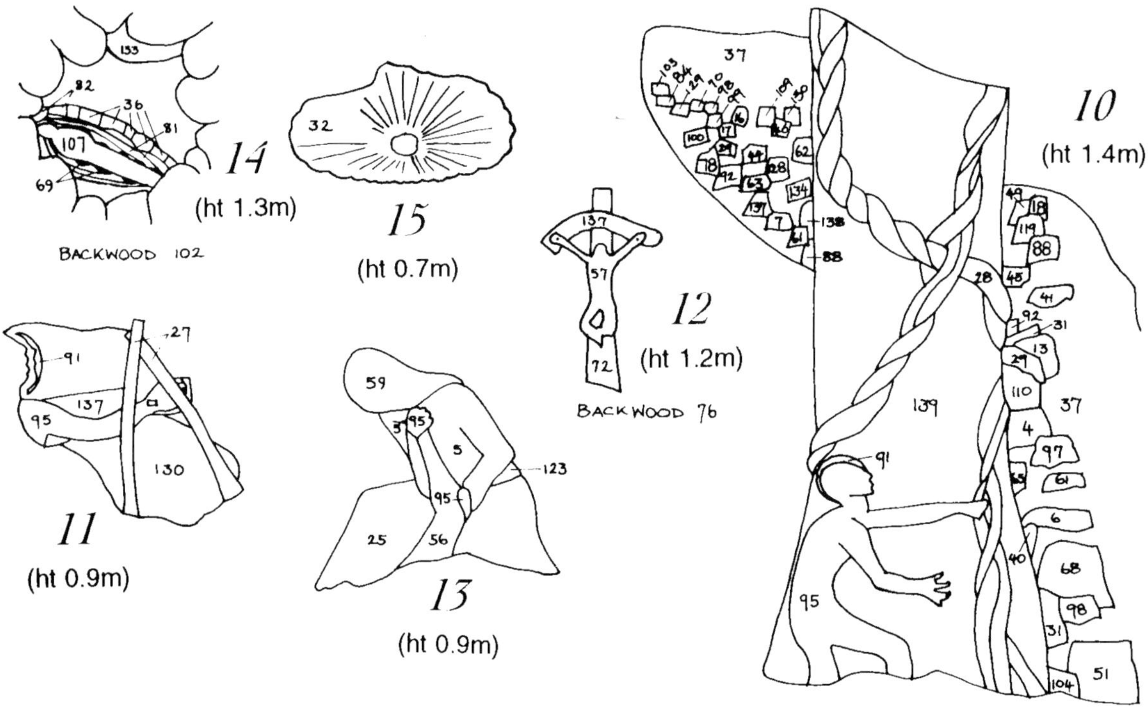

No.	Wood Name	Latin Name	Country of Origin of this Sample	Station Nos
1	AFARA	Terminalia superba	West Africa	*3.5.8.*
2	ALDER	Alnus glutinosa	England	*5.8.*
3	ALMOND	Prunus dulcis	Italy	*8.*
4	ANINGERIA	Aningeria altissima	E & W Africa	*10.*
5	ASH European	Flaxinus excelsior	England	*1.3.4.5.7.8.13.*
6	ASH Olive	Flaxinus excelsior	England	*5.7.8.10.*
7	ASH Japanese	Fraxinus mandschurica	South East Asia	*7.8.10.*
8	ASH Silver	Flindersia schottiana	Queensland, Australia	*1.3.9.*
9	ASPEN	Populus tremuloides	USA & Canada	*7.8.*
10	AU	Hibiscus tiliatenceus	Rarotonga	*8.*
11	AVODIRE	Turraeanthus africanus	West Africa	*1.8.*
12	AYAN	Distemonathus benthamianus	West Africa	*8.*
13	BUBINGA	Guibourtia demeusei	West Africa	*8.10.*
14	BEECH European	Fagus sylvatica	England	*2.3.7.8.*
15	BEECH Red	Nothafagus fusca	New Zealand	*7.8.9.*
16	BEECH Silver	Nothofagus Menziesii	New Zealand	*8.9.10.*
17	BLACKBEAN	Castanospermum australe	E Australia	*8.10.*
18	BLACKWOOD	Acacia melanoxylon	Tasmania Australia	*8.9.10.*
19	BLACKWOOD	Dalbergia melanoxylon	E Africa	*7.8.*
20	BOXWOOD European	Buxus sempervirens	England	*8.*
21	BRUZOLLI		Italy	*8.*
22	CASTELO	Gossypiospermum praecox	South America	*1.3.7.8.*
23	CEDAR Eastern red	Juniperis virguniae	Canada	*8.*
24	CEDAR of Lebanon	Cedrus lebani	England	*5.7.8.*
25	CHERRY American	Prunus serotina	England	*7.13.*
26	CHESTNUT Sweet	Castanea sateva	England	*1.6.8.*

27	COCUS	Brya ebenus	West Indies	*11.*
28	CUCHARILLO	Talauma spp.	Ecuador	*7.10.*
29	DOUGLAS FIR	Pseudotsuga menziesii	USA & Canada	*5.8.10.*
30	EBONY Africa	Diospyrus crassiflora	Africa	*6.7.*
31	EBONY Macassa	Diospyros celebica	Celebes Islands	*2.5.7.8.9.10.*
32	ELM English	Ulmus spp.	England	*4.8.15.*
33	ELM burr	Ulmus spp.	England	*8.*
34	EUCALYPTUS	Eucalyptus spp.	Australia	*9.*
35	FIJI WOOD		Fiji	*8.*
36	FOSSILIZED WOOD	Lignum rupes	New Zealand	*14.*
37	GEDU NOHOR	Entandrophragma angolense	Nigeria	*10.*
38	GREEK WOOD		Greece	*8.*
39	GRENDILLO	Delbergia grenadillo	Central America	*1.7.8.*
40	INDIAN SILVER GRAY		India	*10.*
41	IMBUIA (Brazilian Walnut)	Phoebe porosa	Brazil	*5.8.10.*
42	IROKO	Chlorophora excelsa	West & East Africa	*5.7.9.*
43	IRONWOOD	Olea capensis	Africa	*8.*
44	JARRAH	Eucalypyus marginata	Australian	*5.8.9.10.*
45	JUERAMA			*8.10.*
46	KAHIKATEA	Podocarpus dacrydiodies	New Zealand	*8.9.10.*
47	KANUKA	Leptospermum ericoides	New Zealand	*8.*
48	KAURI PINE	Agathis australis	New Zealand	*7.8.9.*
49	KAURI PINE	Agathis spp.	Fiji	*8.10.*
50	KEVASINGO (rotary cut Bubinga)	Guigourtia demeusei	West Africa	*1.7.8.*
51	KINGWOOD	Dalbergia cearensis	Brazil	*7.10.*
52	KOHEKOHE	Dysoxylum spectabile	New Zealand	*8.9.*
53	LABURNUM	Laburnum anagyroides	England	*8.*
54	LAUREL	Terminalia alata	India/Burma	*7.8.*
55	LIGNUM VITAE	Guaiacum officinale	West Indies	*7.*
56	LIME	Tilia vulgaris	England	*15.*
57	LIME burr	Tilia vulgaris	England	*12.*
58	MAGNOLIA	Magnolia grandiflora	USA	*7.*
59	MAHOE Blue	Hibiscus elatus	Jamaica/W Indies	*15.*
60	MAKORE	Tieghemella heckelii	West Africa	*1.2.5.*
61	MAHOGANY	Swietenia macrophylla	South America	*7.8.10.*
62	MANGEAO	Litsea calicaris	New Zealand	*8.9.10.*
63	MAPLE Australian	Flinderisa brayleyana	Australia & PNG	*8.9.10.*
64	MAPLE burr	Acer spp.	Canada	*5.*
65	MAPLE Rock (birdseye)	Acer saccharum	Canada & USA	*1.5.6.8.10.*
66	MIRO Heart	Thespesia populuea	Rarotonga	*8.*
67	MIRO Sap	Thespesia populuea	Rarotonga	*8.*
68	MULBERRY	Morus nigra	Europe	*10.*
69	MYRRH	Commiphora myrrha	Oman	*14.*
70	MYRTLE BEECH	Nothofagus cunninghamii	Australia	*8.9.10.*
71	OAK Bog	Quercus spp.	England	*7.8.9.*
72	OAK Bog	Quercus spp. (5000 yrs old)	Ireland	*12.*
73	OAK Brown	Quercus robur	England	*1.7.*
74	OAK Burr	Quercus robur	England	*5.7.8.*
75	OAK Cork	Quercus suber	Greece	*8.*
76	OAK European	Quercus robur	England	*2.12.*
77	OAK Red	Quercus rubra	France	*8.*
78	OAK Silky	Cardwellia sublimis	Australia	*1.3.5.7.9.10.*
79	OAK Tiger	Quercus robur	England	*6.7.*
80	OLIVE European	Olea europaea	Italy	*6.8.*
81	OLIVE	Olea europaea	Bethlehem	*14.*
82	OLIVE	Olea europaea	Jerusalem	*14.*
83	OLIVE (tropical)	Olea hochstetteri	East Africa	*7.8.*

84	OPEPE	Nauclea diderrichii	West Africa	*8.10.*
85	OSAGE ORANGE	Maclura pomifera	New Zealand	*8.*
86	PADUAK African	Pterocarpus soyauxii	Central & W Africa	*1.3.5.7.*
87	PADAUK Andaman	Pterocarpus dalbergioides	Andaman Islands	*8.*
88	PALDAO	Dracontomelum dao	Philippines	*3.8.10.*
89	PALM Coconut	Cocos nucifera	Indonesia	*7.8.*
90	PEAR	Pyrus communis	France	*8.*
91	PEQUIA	Aspidospema eberneum	Brazil	*1.2.3.4.5.6.7.8.9.10.11.*
92	PINE Scots	Pinus sylvestris	Eastern Europe /Russia	*7.8.10.*
93	PINE Silver	Dacrydium colensoi	New Zealand	*7.9.*
94	PINK IVORY	Rhamnus zeyheri	S & SE Africa	*8.*
95	PLANE European (lacewood)	Platanus acerifolia	England	*1.2.3.4.5.6.7.8.9.10.11.13.*
96	PLUM		India	*8.*
97	PURPLEHEART	Peltogyne spp.	South America	*2.5.7.8.10.*
98	RAMIN	Gonystylus macrophyllum	SE Asia	*8.9.10.*
99	RATA	Metrosideros robusta	New Zealand	*8.9.10.*
100	REWA REWA	Knightia excelsa	New Zealand	*8.9.10.*
101	RIBBONWOOD (Honeria)	Hoheria populnea	New Zealand	*8.9.*
102	RIMU heart	Dacrydium cupressinum	New Zealand	*7.9.14.*
103	RIMU sap	Dacrydium cupressinum	New Zealand	*8.9.10.*
104	ROSEWOOD Brazilian	Dalbergia nigra	South America	*5.7.8.10.*
105	ROSEWOOD Indian	Dalbergia latifolia	India	*3.5.7.8.*
106	SABRIANNE		Italy	*2.7.8.*
107	SANDALWOOD	Santalum album	India	*14.*
108	SANDON			*2.3.*
109	SANGRAGON		New Guinea	*3.8.9.10.*
110	SANTOS		South America	*8.10.*
111	SAPELE Birdseye	Entandrophragma cylindricum	East &West Africa	*1.2.3.5.8.*
112	SATIN WOOD	Chloroxylon swietenia	Sri Lanka	*7.8.*
113	SEE SAM		India	*8.*
114	STINKWOOD (Laurel)	Ocotea bullata	South Africa	*8.*
115	SYCAMORE pink dyed	Acer pseudoplatanus	England	*2.*
116	SYCAMORE weathered	Acer pseudoplatanus	England	*7.8.*
117	TAMANU	Calophyllium inophyllium	Rarotonga	*5.*
118	TAWA	Beilschmeidia tawa	New Zealand	*9.*
119	TEAK	Tectona grandis	Burma/Thailand	*8.10.*
120	TOTARA	Podocarpus totara	New Zealand	*7.*
121	TOTARA bog	Podocarpus totara	New Zealand	*9.*
122	TOU	Cordia subcordata	Raratonga	*7.8.*
123	TSIPATY		Madagasca	*13.*
124	TULIP	Liriodendron tulipifera	Brazil	*8.*
125	TULIP	Liriodendron tulipifera	England	*8.*
126	UTILE	Entandrophragma utile	Ivory Coast /Ghana	*8.*
127	WALNUT African	Lovoa trichilioides	Nigeria	*5.*
128	WALNUT Black American	Juglans nigra	USA & Canada	*2.7.8.10.*
129	WALNUT Eastern	Endiandra Palmerstonii	New Caledonia	*8.9.10.*
130	WALNUT European	Juglans regia	England	*7.8.10.11.*
131	WALNUT burr	Juglans regia	England	*3.7.8.*
132	WALNUT Queensland	Engiandra palmerstonii	Australia	*8.9.*
133	WELLINGTONIA	Sequioadendron giganteum	New Zealand	*8.14.*
134	WENGE	Millettia spp.	West Africa	*10.*
135	WHITEWOOD		Fiji	*8.9.*
136	WILLOW	Salix alba	England	*8.*
137	YEW	Taxus baccata	England	*1.2.3.4.5.6.7.8.9.10.11.12.*
138	ZEBRANO	Hicroberlinia brazzauillensis	Africa	*3.5.7.8.10.*
139	ZIRICOTE	Cordia dodecandra	Belize	*10.*